Smile Southern California, You're the Center of the Universe

The Economy and People of a Global Region

James Flanigan

With a Foreword by Richard Riordan

STANFORD GENERAL BOOKS
An Imprint of Stanford University Press
Stanford, California

Stanford University Press
Stanford, California

Printed in the United States of America on acid-free, archival-quality paper

Library of Congress Cataloging-in-Publication Data
Flanigan, James, 1936–
 Smile Southern California, you're the center of the universe : the economy and people of a global region / James Flanigan ; with a foreword by Richard Riordan.
     p. cm.
 Includes bibliographical references and index.
 ISBN 978-0-8047-5625-9 (cloth : alk. paper)
     1. California, Southern—Economic conditions.   2. California, Southern—Commerce.
     3. Business enterprises—California, Southern.   4. Globalization—California,
Southern.   I. Title.
 HC107.C22F53 2009
 330.9794'9—dc22
              2008042795

Typeset by Bruce Lundquist in 11/15 Bell MT

Special discounts for bulk quantities of Stanford General Books are available to corporations, professional associations, and other organizations. For details and discount information, contact the special sales department of Stanford University Press. Tel: (650) 736-1783, Fax: (650) 736-1784

Contents

Foreword

I ADMIRED JIM FLANIGAN as a business columnist with the *Los Angeles Times* and, later, as a member of my book club. Personally, he is a great comedian, an intellect, and most of all a curmudgeon. His book is the first to tell all about Los Angeles' great economy—the past, the present, and the future. Readers will be surprised at the industries in which Los Angeles is number one in the United States.

I was flattered when Jim asked me to write this foreword, although he criticized my first draft for being too cerebral: "People want to hear about Dick Riordan—they don't like this humility crap." Well, you asked for it Jim, and here I go.

I grew up in New York, where your life depended on how expertly you dodged automobiles. My first memory of Los Angeles is from October 9, 1956, when I took my first steps onto Sunset Boulevard. I remember how every car stopped to let me cross—a rare occurrence nowadays, but nonetheless, a great welcoming experience to the place I would call home for the next fifty-two years. It never would have occurred to me that I would be its mayor for two terms.

All my adult life I had dreamed of living in California, with its magnificent beaches, mountains, and open living style. I wasn't disappointed—I had made Shangri-La my home.

I was twenty-six years old and had just graduated from the University of Michigan Law School when the prestigious Los Angeles law firm O'Melveny & Myers recruited me to the West Coast. My salary was $350 per month—not bad for those days. Today, young lawyers start at $13,000 per month (wow!). My wife and I paid $105 per month for a furnished two-bedroom apartment. We lived so well on my salary that we were able to afford two $3 dinners at Monty's Steak House once a month.

My first case at O'Melveny was to represent homeowners in Portuguese Bend, a small community on a hill inside the Palos Verdes Peninsula just south of Los Angeles. Their homes were (and still are) sliding down the hill as a result of the county government excavating with millions of gallons of water for an extension of Crenshaw Avenue, some five miles from Portuguese Bend. Proving negligence was difficult because we probably could not prove foreseeability. But I came up with the then-unique concept of inverse condemnation; that is, the government is liable for actions that cause a decrease in the value of property the same as if they had taken the property. Little did I realize that inverse condemnation would result in billions of dollars of judgments against cities and states for many years.

In addition to my position as junior lawyer with O'Melveny & Myers, I was often "lent out" as an executive assistant on civic projects, such as the annual meeting of the American Bar Association, Town Hall, United Way, and the Catholic archdiocese. These experiences introduced me to Los Angeles' most powerful and influential families—many of whom were directly involved in building Los Angeles into a great city, rather than just a bunch of "suburbs in search of a city." Then, it seemed as if overnight we had the Music Center, the MOCA and Getty museums, the Sports Arena, freeways, and high-rise buildings. The pseudo suburbs of Encino, Boyle Heights, Brentwood, Bel Air, Pacific Palisades, Watts, Van Nuys, etc., were brought together.

It's interesting that if you dig a little deeper and research some of these Los Angeles icons—many of whom rightfully have parks, schools, and streets named after them—you'll find that they were the descendants of devious minds. For instance, oil tycoon Edward L. Doheny was accused of bribing Secretary of the Interior Albert Fall in the Teapot Dome Scandal of the 1920s (his acquittal was just as surprising as that of O. J. Simpson), and *Los Angeles Times* publisher Harry Chandler was involved in the water and real estate scandals that inspired the 1974 Roman Polanski film *Chinatown*.

Their descendants were among my mentors and were great, ethical leaders, including Otis Chandler, who turned the *Los Angeles Times* into a newspaper of national prominence, and members of the Doheny family, whose achievements included founding Mount St. Mary's College and Immaculate Heart College.

As a young lawyer, I befriended many of the city's future magnates, including Eli Broad, Cardinal Roger Mahony, Harold Williams, Rob Maguire, Steve Soboroff, Bruce Karatz, Lew Wasserman, Arnold Schwarzenegger, Robert Lowe, Warren Christopher, Julian Burke, and Frank Gehry. These are the ones who added such great treasures to Los Angeles as the Disney Concert Hall, the Staples Center, the new cathedral, and the Getty Museum, as well as major shopping centers, homeless drop-in centers, and the Alameda Corridor. As Claremont Colleges economist Peter Drucker said, "All great projects start in the mind and the heart of a single individual." Los Angeles has had more than its fair share of such individuals. I attribute my successes as mayor (1993–2001) to these friendships and many others along the way. I accept accolades not for being brilliant, but for demonstrating brilliance in my ability to empower my staff and network of friends and acquaintances to make great things happen.

A lot of people have asked me why I ran for mayor of Los Angeles at a time when the city was at its lowest point, with soaring crime rates, the first economic recession in its history, and the Rodney King riots. Angelinos had lost their confidence, and the national media had fun tearing us apart. All my life I've been a problem solver with an addiction for filling vacancies. The soon-to-retire mayor, Tom Bradley, and the chief of police, Daryl Gates, had not spoken to each other in two years. Mayor Bradley, who deservedly gets most of the credit for the expansion of Los Angeles, had lost interest. Corporate lawyer and venture capitalist Bill Wardlaw talked me into running and oversaw my campaign. After being beat up in the media for all kinds of imaginative crimes (Bill's advice: "Keep your mouth shut"), I won by eight percentage points—not bad for a rich, white Republican in a three-to-one Democratic city.

When the Disney family spent $50 million on the Disney Concert Hall with no plans to raise the $300 million needed to complete it, I summoned my close friends Eli Broad and architect Frank Gehry to the challenge. Eli and I often rode bikes and hiked through the Santa Monica Mountains, while Frank and I joked that we were the oldest hockey players in the world. The decision to resurrect the concert hall was made after Frank blindsided me during an ice hockey game. As I got up from the ice in pain, Frank gave me his evil smile and said, "Let's make up and make Disney Hall happen." Through Eli Broad's leadership, we raised $300 million, and Frank designed what is perhaps the greatest architectural masterpiece of the past century. I was proud that I brought these two great men together; in fact, until then, they hadn't talked to each other in ten years.

People joked that I was an expert at empowering others and then taking credit for what they did. Actually, there is a lot of truth in this. I am not a man who claims to have all the answers; I simply know where and how to find them. There is no problem for which I cannot find an expert to solve it: Eli Broad and Frank Gehry made Disney Concert Hall happen; Steve Soboroff made Staples Sports Center and the Alameda Corridor happen; Bruce Karatz made the first homeless drop-in center in the country and the computerization of the Los Angeles Police Department happen; Julian Burke, who made a fortune restructuring Penn Central Railroad and other companies, turned the stagnant Metropolitan Transit Authority around; Bob Lowe rolled out a marketing program that turned around the nation's opinion about Los Angeles; and on and on.

Perhaps the biggest lesson I learned was on January 17, 1994, when I was knocked out of bed at 4:31 a.m. by the Northridge earthquake. I immediately reached for the phone, only to find silence on the other end. No dial tone. I pulled on the first pair of sweatpants I could find and jumped in my car, heading for the Emergency Operations Center four stories below City Hall, which was fifteen miles from my home. Driving down the vacant Santa Monica Freeway at ninety miles per hour through the early morning darkness, I was suddenly stunned by two bright lights heading straight for me. I swerved slightly and hit the brakes to avoid a large truck heading down the wrong side of the freeway. I soon realized that the truck had saved me from sailing off the collapsed bridge over La Cienega Boulevard. I looked at the bridge debris, did a U-turn, and cautiously drove back on the wrong side of the freeway to the nearest exit. Fortunately, no other cars were on the freeway.

At 5:05 a.m., I arrived at City Hall and descended the four floors to the Emergency Operations Center, where there were cubicles for forty of the city departments plus rooms for the police and fire departments. Bob Yates, my head of transportation, arrived moments later, and together, we assessed the damage and discussed detours around the five fallen freeway bridges. The only reasonable detour around the bridge over La Cienega included three intersections in Culver City. Bob explained that before we took over these intersections, state law and regulations required that environmental studies, traffic mitigation reports, actions by both city councils, and more had to happen. The Santa Monica Freeway is the busiest and economically most important road in the United States. We couldn't wait. At that moment, heaven inspired what is now called Riordan's first Law: "It is much easier to get forgiveness than to get permission—so just do it!" I told Bob he had ten minutes to take over the intersections, and if anyone complained, he was to give them my home telephone number. No one called. I never had to ask for forgiveness.

The morning after the quake, I met with California governor Pete Wilson and executives of the California Department of Transportation in the governor's Los Angeles conference room. I learned that state law or regulations required that we use Caltrans state employees to repair the damaged bridges. I asked them whether they had architects and engineers looking at the bridges on the day of the earthquake. It took almost an hour for these bureaucrats to admit that they didn't, but they had plans to do so. It took another half hour for them to admit that they didn't know when they would implement these plans. Meanwhile, each day the bridges went unrepaired cost the city of Los Angeles and its citizens more than $25 million. I asked the governor's chief of transportation, Dean Dumphy, and the head of federal highways, Rod Slater, to adjourn with me outside the conference room, where I lost my temper, yelling: "Those sons of &#@$% bureaucrats are playing mind $#!@ing games with us. Let's get private architects and engineering firms at the fallen bridge sites this afternoon." From there, Dumphy picked up the ball and carried it over the goal line. Within one day we hired private contractors to repair the bridges and included bonus offerings for every day under three months that it took to complete the project. The bridges were all repaired in sixty-six days.

It had taken San Francisco and Caltrans more than fourteen years to repair freeways after the 1989 Loma Prieta earthquake. But San Fran learned a lesson from Los Angeles and repaired in record time the 2007 damage to the Bay Bridge caused by a tanker explosion. My good friends at the *Los Angeles Times* criticized us for paying the bonuses—"Long Live Bureaucracy!"

I've learned many lessons throughout my years both as mayor of Los Angeles and as a private investor. Along with "It is much easier to get forgiveness . . . ," I also remember: "Don't do other people's thinking for them"; "I couldn't agree with you more"; "Empower others and give them credit"; "Beware of immediate reactions"; "Only a mediocre person never makes a mistake"; and while you're at it, "Beware of committees, working groups, and consultants." Most of all: "Children above bureaucrats" and "Just do it!"

Now, turn the page and learn from Jim Flanigan about the secrets of what makes Los Angeles a great city, and what some of its entrepreneurial stories can teach us about business today and the economy at large.

Richard Riordan
Former mayor of Los Angeles

Preface

Southern California was discovered from the east, by
westward moving migrants. Looked at from its eastern
approaches the region could not be seen in proper
perspective; its significance remained obscure. But when
one approaches the region from across the Pacific, it begins
to assume an altogether different aspect. The sense of
detachment from the rest of the continent gives way to a
feeling of its integral relation to the rest of the Pacific world.

Carey McWilliams,
Southern California: An Island on the Land, 1946

SUPERMARKET OWNER DARIOUSH KHALEDI went to
survey damage at one of his stores in Compton, California, the day after riots had torn through the south Los Angeles area
in 1992. He had resolved to close the store because of the damages and
evident danger in the neighborhood. He was gloomy about the prospect as the riot was the first setback to the company that Khaledi and
his brother-in-law, Paul Vazin, immigrants from Iran who didn't speak
much English, had started in 1977. K. V. Mart Co., which catered to minority customers from Latin America and the Caribbean, had succeeded
like an American dream, growing to fourteen stores and more than two
hundred employees. Now, as he neared the battered store, Khaledi saw a
crowd advancing across the parking lot. He looked at them in surprise.
The people were carrying brooms, buckets, and sponges. They had been

waiting to help him clean up. "We reopened that store in eight days," Khaledi recalled in 1996.[1] So the dream lived on. Today, K. V. Mart has twenty-two stores in Los Angeles and Orange and Ventura counties.

Southern California is like that: unpredictable, perplexing, and vibrant. This region is at the nexus of Latin America and Asia, and in the past two decades it has opened up to economic opportunity, population growth, and enormous energy from those continents. Southern California today embodies a great shift in the United States to an economy driven by international commerce and entrepreneurial business and finance. It is an economy that receives people and investment from around the world and that is constantly renewed by changing technology. With 22 million people and a yearly output of goods and services (gross regional product) equal to or greater than that of India, Brazil, Russia, or Mexico, the half-dozen counties of Southern California lead a transformation of the U.S. economy.[2]

The changes of this era are comparable to those of the post–World War II period, when America moved to a national economy, distributing merchandise over interstate highways and advertising its wares on television. Los Angeles emerged into national consciousness at that time. Today, the move is to a global economy and the extraordinary communications revolution of the Internet.

I have reported on Southern California for almost forty years for *Forbes* magazine, the *Los Angeles Times,* and the *New York Times.* I have seen the region with a sassy sense of itself in the late 1960s, when a billboard over Olympic Boulevard advertised a radio station with the tongue-in-cheek greeting, "Smile Los Angeles, You're the Center of the Universe." I have seen it at the depth of economic depression and doubt in the early 1990s, when the aerospace-defense industry cut back and went away. And I have seen the region rise again with new industries and people. That local knowledge gives me the wherewithal to write this book. But it is my perspective gained from reporting across the globe that inspires me to write it. I have seen economic progress amid tremendous challenges in countries—such as Japan, Israel, and Ireland—that created economies based on knowledge work. I have seen hidden flaws amid seeming economic might in the Soviet Union, the Shah's Iran, Saddam's Iraq, and much else of the Middle East. And I have seen the struggle for human improvement that goes on in South Africa, Mexico, and China and in towns and regions across the United States.

I believe that all places of great change combine seeming chaos and positive development if energetic people are given education and freedom to improve their lives. Today, Southern California is just that kind of place, confronting challenges of poverty amid wealth, poor education and young people at risk, industrial growth, and environmental damage. The area in a sense has always been like that—and *always* for this region has not been a long, long time. Rather, Southern California is a new place, populated mainly during the past century and built in a hurry by energetic businesspeople and boosters who saw their opportunities in the area's climate and fertility—and took them! That boosterish strain begat in turn a critical reaction, first among writers like Upton Sinclair, James M. Cain, and Raymond Chandler, who spotted evil under the palm fronds and created a noir tradition in books and brooding movies such as *Double Indemnity* and *Farewell, My Lovely*.

The noir tradition carried over to scholarly commentary in recent decades after the growth and promise of the 1950s and 1960s turned complex and blotchy in later decades. Author Mike Davis, prominently, wrote of disintegrating social fabric and declining economic vitality in his books *City of Quartz: Excavating the Future of Los Angeles* (1990) and *Ecology of Fear: Los Angeles and the Imagination of Disaster* (1998). He saw changes occurring at the end of the 1980s, including cutbacks in defense spending and increases in Japanese trade and investment, as foreshadowing decline. To be sure, those were troubled times, and today's environment is no picnic. But the forebodings were not borne out. The changes that came to Southern California in the 1990s turned out far better than most people predicted.

A new economy emerged from seeds planted during the old. This is the very point of this book. I don't deny there are problems; indeed, formidable challenges confront this region. Los Angeles has spectacular problems, including 250 street gangs with twenty-six thousand members, according to the Los Angeles Police Department. The gangs have committed more than twenty-three thousand serious crimes in the past five years. Today's Southern California is no Oneida Community, no Shining City on a Hill. But it is a dynamic region emblematic of changes in the United States and the world. My book takes off from the downturn of the early 1990s and follows the emergence of an entrepreneurial economy that in many ways is more democratic than plutocratic. The Southern California economy of this decade—even amid present worries about a global recession—has greater variety of work and lower unemployment than in previous times. The shift in ethnic makeup throughout the region, while not without tensions, is proceeding far better than many foresaw. In private industry and government service up and down California, immigrants and their children and grandchildren are taking their places in the mainstream of American society at a pace that mirrors and often improves upon that of earlier decades and centuries of our history.

That is my perspective, optimistic perhaps, but no more so than the reasoned optimism of other students of California, such as historian Kevin Starr, *Coast of Dreams* (2004); author Peter Schrag, *California: America's High Stakes Experiment* (2006); urban historian Joel Kotkin, *The City* (2005); and the University of California, Irvine, scholars Rob Kling, Spencer Olin, and Mark Poster, whose *Postsuburban California* (1995) describes Orange County as a new landscape, one that characterizes so many urban areas of contemporary America. In short, I focus on the enterprise and achievements of the region's people, businesses, and institutions because the achievements are substantial and they're linked to historic developments in the world economy.

A New Paradigm

In this book I tell the stories of people, companies, and industries in order to illustrate the global developments affecting our economies and our lives. The first three—of eight—chapters explain the characteristics of Southern California's economy that make it a model for the United States and the world. first, there is international trade, which is now a leading contributor to the U.S. gross national product in a world economy swelled by billions of new participants—principally the enormous populations of Asia, Latin America, and Eastern Europe. In today's global trade, however, industries and countries do not merely exchange goods and services but collaborate in *producing* them. This is a new paradigm and a richer exchange. The ideas behind products and services are the most valuable factors in the process; concept and design count for more than simple manufacture. This is hardly revolutionary. The engineers who designed the automobiles have always been more highly compensated than the assembly line workers who put them together.

But we have entered a new age in which work and production are decentralized, employing many actors in a unified drama. In this new world, global businesses do not practice simple arts of export and import but the complex tasks of "supply chain management" and "framework architecture," words taken from the realm of information technology that simply mean assigning specific responsibilities to many and separate parts in a global process. The need and idea for a product may originate in one country, say, the United States, and its fabrication may occur in another, say, China, after which it is shipped back to the United States and distributed and sold there. Or a product or service may remain in China and be sold there, or China may seek to open a plant in the United States to make and sell its products here and gain a larger share of the proceeds. All these transactions are happening every day now, yet they are not broadly understood by the general public and there is frequent outcry that "China (or India) makes everything, we make nothing anymore." Chapter 1 seeks to banish such misconceptions by explaining, through examples of companies and individuals, how the world works today and why Southern California became preeminent in the nation's trade.

Significantly, Chapter 1 notes that the rapid rise of international trade in the past decade has not occurred merely because China is a large and populous country or because the Cold War ended in 1989. Trade rose to today's proportions because of the spreading use of the Internet for commerce and other purposes by individuals and organizations the world over. Southern California was present at its creation. In Chapter 2, I tell of four scientists at the University of California, Los Angeles (UCLA) who, working in collaboration with researchers at the University of California, Santa Barbara; Stanford Research Institute; and the University of Utah, "invented" the Internet on a project for the Defense Department. The Pentagon was seeking to create a totally distributed communications system, with no command centers that could be vulnerable in time of war. The ARPANET (Advanced Research Projects Agency

Network) was created from UCLA's research and was the forerunner of today's Internet. Also, the basic scientific and technological principles that later created cellular telephony and wireless Internet communication were developed at UCLA and at the University of California, San Diego, in the 1970s and 1980s.

Those discoveries, which began with financial support from the Defense Department, were profound for Southern California and the broader U.S. economy. They led to the industrial environment we know to this day in which small companies can operate and innovate as well as large corporations, and often better. The Internet and inexpensive wireless communications are remaking the world as we speak, with computing and entertainment gravitating to mobile phone systems and new possibilities opening up. Chapter 2 also explains how significant it is that after initial Pentagon funding, companies and breakthroughs of the new age are financed primarily by entrepreneurial, decentralized investment rather than the federal government, as was the case during the postwar era in Southern California.

Chapter 3 explores the shift in finance to a modern economy that stresses innovation and entrepreneurial vigor. A half century ago, Southern California had many potential entrepreneurs, but it was almost impossible for them to attract financing for new businesses. Simon Ramo and Dean Wooldridge, whose names are behind two of the initials in TRW Inc., were brilliant engineers at the time, but nobody would back them on their own. Instead, prevailing industrial thinking and the Pentagon married them to a Cleveland auto parts company named Thompson because that represented better collateral. Yet the atmosphere changed profoundly during the 1980s when venture financing, backed by family and pension trust investors, came into vogue. In Southern California, Michael Milken turned conventional wisdom on its head and sparked a spread of credit to innovative new companies. Everywhere, the corporate landscape was altered, albeit not always without pain. Chapter 3 explains crises that have recurred in Asia and in the U.S. economy because of distortions of finance and overexpansion of credit. But the chapter also explores the underlying reality of this age, in which Asia and Latin America are joining and expanding the ranks of developed industrial countries. This global expansion offers far more possibilities than pitfalls for America and the rest of the world. Chapter 3 acknowledges another shift, as Southern California has blossomed with newcomers from Korea and India, Vietnam and China, Mexico and Central America, and elsewhere. Southern California became the new Ellis Island and reaped economic energy as immigrants started businesses. "These people did not come all the way from Asia to work for a salary," observed one banker. "They came to build businesses. They were not thinking of retirement plans but of new adventures." Chapter 3 discusses several of these immigrant communities, their different approaches to business, and their contributions to the new mosaic in Southern California and the United States.

Immigration and Arrival

Chapters 4 and 5 focus on two significant groups of newcomers: the Latinos—with origins mainly in Mexico—and the Chinese. Chapter 4 explains the importance of this historic period of immigration for the U.S. economy and highlights the rising economic, social, and political role of Latino people in the American mosaic. It discusses the realities of fraught questions about illegal immigration and outlines the kinds of solutions that will be coming in the next few years as a new national administration takes office in 2009. The chapter also points out that both Latinos and recent Chinese arrivals now are less immigrant groups than emergent middle-class populations in the American mainstream. By explaining some history and profiling individuals and companies in the Latino and Chinese communities, these chapters examine businesses and individuals who are having a widening effect on the U.S. economy. Chapter 5 profiles individuals in the Chinese American community, showing how success in Southern California is creating new ventures in China. The chapter tells also of efforts to spread knowledge of Chinese culture in America and to adapt philosophies of the ancient sages Confucius and Lao-tzu to U.S. business practices.

Chapters 6 and 7 discuss new demands placed on two institutions in the Southern California economy: universities and entertainment. Both are undergoing profound change thanks to new technologies and the larger global economy. Chapter 6 focuses on universities and their role as performers of long-term research for the U.S. economy. Bell

Laboratories once did scientific research, and the Defense Department for decades financed basic science, but such efforts now are entrusted to university departments financed by contributions from corporations and government agencies. Southern California's great phalanx of institutions, including five campuses of the University of California system, the California Institute of Technology, and the University of Southern California, are in the vanguard of pooling resources on important projects. Chapter 6 shows how every university, spurred by federal law and the hope of revenue, is stepping up efforts to transfer access to new technologies to private industry and the general public.

Chapter 7 illustrates how a founding industry of Southern California, film and television production, is now both threatened by new Internet-based technologies and offered greatly expanded horizons. Plans and strategies of Southern California companies indicate the way the world is turning both in transitions to online media and in the movement beyond exporting of films and television shows to collaborative ventures in China, India, and other countries.

Finally, Chapter 8 analyzes how Southern California proposes to meet the challenges of mobility and infrastructure, environmental accommodation, education, and social harmony for a greatly expanding and diverse population in the coming decades. The chapter explains how new models of public-private partnerships are being proposed to meet the needs for expanded infrastructure of ports, airports, roads, and water systems in times of straitened municipal and state budgets. It examines the continuing crises of subpar public schools and high dropout rates for students from poor and immigrant populations, as well as what solutions are being devised and put into practice. It looks at interracial tensions in Southern California's extraordinarily polyglot populations but does so with perspective. Today's global economy, with its pervasive effects throughout the region, opens more opportunities for young people and thereby serves to ease potential problems. Also, despite undeniable problems caused by ethnic gangs, Southern California visibly takes a certain pride in its diversity these days, proclaiming itself as a new model for America. And so it is. In assimilating new groups, as in pioneering new models for industry, Southern California provides a beacon for the entire country.

Carey McWilliams's landmark 1949 book was called *California: The Great Exception*. But today, that concept is out of date. California, north and south, is the dynamic model of a Pacific-centered world. Southern California is no longer the exception, but rather the example that lights the future.

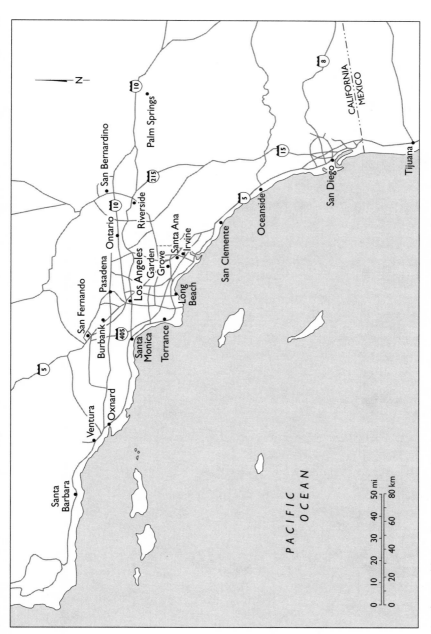

Southern California, from Santa Barbara to the border of Mexico and from the Pacific Ocean to San Bernardino, Riverside, and the eastern edges of Los Angeles, Ventura, and Santa Barbara counties. Map by William L. Nelson

1   Global Trade, Local Industry

The evidence is overwhelmingly persuasive that the massive
increase in world competition—a consequence of broadening
trade flows—has fostered markedly higher standards of living
for almost all countries who have participated in cross-border
trade. I include most especially the United States.

Alan Greenspan,

speech, Boston, June 2, 1999

C HINA, JAPAN, AND SOUTH KOREA engaged in $268
billion worth of merchandise trade with the ports of
Los Angeles and Long Beach in 2007. Mexico and countries in Central
America traded $67.6 billion worth of goods through the San Diego
customs district during that period. The totals are at historic levels.[1]

What these statistics reveal is that the United States has a new *kind*
of economy, one more heavily involved in international trade, particularly
with nations in Asia and Latin America. These continents are coming
to the fore thanks to changing technology and the added participation
of hundreds of millions of people in the global economy. *Globalization*
is the name given to this historic shift, and it is more responsible than
any other factor for Southern California's emergence as a center of the
U.S. and world economies. Geography plays a role; the region's location looking west to Asia and south to Mexico and Central and South
America put it in the path of development. Also, it's the people's choice:
Southern California in the past two decades has become the leading

destination for immigrants from Latin America and Asia.[2] But it is in industry that Southern California has prepared for this new eminence. In the past eighteen years, the region has spawned new industries, reformed old ones, and served as a beacon for a new economy led by hundreds of thousands of small to medium-sized companies.

A global economy is not built in a day. A century and more of work

Figure 1.1. The main channel at the Port of Los Angeles, which adjoins the Port of Long Beach to make up the largest port complex in the United States. Courtesy of the Port of Los Angeles.

and public investment in seaports and airports prepared the region for this time. And a confluence of developments in technology and of social, political, and economic changes around the world has led to Southern California's global importance. What we are witnessing today is collaboration between the most advanced economy in the world and large, very poor nations that house the populations and the potential to expand the global economy to historic levels. Southern California plays a key role in this collaboration. Businesses in the region have joint production arrangements with companies in Asia and in Mexico. Goods designed in this area or elsewhere in the United States are ordered from producers across the world and come back here through ports in Southern California. Indeed, sometimes electronic and software products are created, designed, and produced simultaneously by people working here and in India or elsewhere in Asia.

I will try to provide an understanding of these processes through the stories of people and relatively small organizations in Southern California. In the past two decades, this vast region of 22 million people, stretching from Santa Barbara to the Mexican border and from the Pacific Ocean to the deserts beyond San Bernardino and Riverside counties, has gone from being an outlying fringe of the U.S. economy to becoming its center. A good place to begin a discussion of trade is with the port complex of Los Angeles and Long Beach that in the past decade has taken its place among the great ports of history, from ancient Nanjing and Calicut to Venice, London, and New York (see Figure 1.1). The Southern California twin ports are now the largest in the United States and, along with Los Angeles International Airport, annually receive more than 45 percent of all the goods that come into the country.[3]

Public-Private Partnership

Los Angeles and Long Beach became the largest ports in the country because of a combination of a business leader's act of will and constant investment, vision, and planning by municipal public agencies commissioned to own and operate great regional assets. Steven Erie's 2004 book *Globalizing L.A.* tells of the campaign led by Harrison Gray Otis, a Civil War veteran who bought a newspaper called the *Los Angeles Daily Times* in 1884, to organize the region's businesspeople in a fight with the Southern Pacific Railroad for the location of a new seaport complex.[4] Otis and local businessmen wanted the port on San Pedro Bay, south of Los Angeles, while the powerful Southern Pacific—with its base at San Francisco—wanted a smaller port facility located on the Pacific at Santa Monica, west of Los Angeles. After a decade-long battle in courts and in the federal and state legislatures in Washington, D.C., and Sacramento, Otis and Southern California business interests prevailed. Work on the harbor began in 1899. After that, the same business interests pushed for municipal and state ownership and control of the harbor because they had a vision of the growth that was to come and the need for public finance to dredge ship channels and develop the port complex. A similar pattern emerged in nearby Long Beach, where a private company developed a port complex but ran out of money in 1915 and was replaced by a municipal port authority. Long Beach has floated bond issues over the decades to finance dredging and upgrading of harbor facilities. Today, the Southern California ports are unique in that they can accommodate container ships from China that carry enormous cargoes in eighty-five hundred individual twenty-ton containers. The ports handled 15.9 million containers in 2007, more than double their load in 2000 (see Figure 1.2).[5]

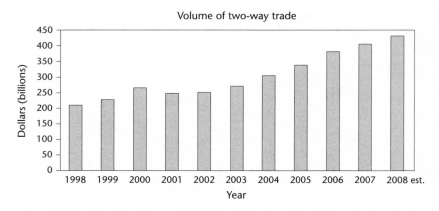

Figure 1.2. Increase in trade through the ports and airports of Southern California through the Los Angeles and San Diego customs districts. Sources: Author's calculations based on U.S. Department of Commerce, U.S. Bureau of the Census, and Los Angeles County Economic Development Corp.

To be sure, the growth of commerce with Asia and Latin America has brought new business and new people to other parts of the United States. The port of New York, historically the nation's leader before the ascendancy of Los Angeles, is seeing greatly increased trade with China and Korea coming through the Suez and Panama canals. New York now boasts that it is an "Asian-dominated port instead of a European one." Immigration has brought new populations and business to other major cities, as well. Miami sees itself as the key entry point for South America; Houston, which has seen a 25 percent population increase to more than 2 million in the past decade, boasts of its ethnic diversity these days. But Los Angeles and Southern California, with more trade, greater population, more immigrants, and more ethnic diversity than other areas, establishes the national trends these days.

In international trade, the ports of entry themselves are only the beginning of a new industry. They feed a transportation complex of trucks, highways, railroads, and warehouses that stretches more than seventy miles to San Bernardino and Riverside counties, an area that's as large as New England. At that point, containers are transferred to rail flatcars that carry the goods throughout the United States and into Canada and Mexico. A leader of the San Bernardino business community, Larry Sharp, president of Arrowhead Credit Union, proudly declared several years ago that the area is a "foreign trade economy." Indeed, he was correct in saying that. All the cargo handling, transportation, and other activities employ more than 650,000 workers, making international trade the largest single source of employment in the Southern California region.[6] Yet even this is not the whole story. The great cascade of merchandise coming through the ports is surpassed in value by the concepts, designs, and intellectual property that originate in Southern California and are beamed via the Internet to production facilities around the Pacific Rim. The number of planners, designers, scientists and engineers, bankers, lawyers and accountants, and other "knowledge employees" engaged in these activities is incalculable.

Simply put, the twenty-first-century trade of this region is a collaborative process, not a mere exchange of imports and exports. Companies in Los Angeles and Orange counties, in San Diego, Santa Barbara, and the grandly named Inland Empire counties of San Bernardino and

Riverside conceive of and design products that are then assembled or augmented partly in Asia, partly back here, and distributed throughout North America. *It is a global production system*, and the base of a thriving new economy. The word *new* is not misplaced. The rise of this trade colossus has occurred in only a few rapid decades. As recently as the 1970s, the ports of Los Angeles and Long Beach were regional shipping points for California's rich agricultural produce plus some machinery and other goods. They handled roughly $16 billion a year in crops, livestock, and manufactures. But then Japanese cars, a response to gasoline scarcity in the 1970s, swelled imports to Los Angeles. And just at that time, the late 1970s, the enlarged global economy started to become a reality.

In 1978, Premier Deng Xiaoping allowed China's farmers to keep some of the income from their labors and eased other central planning restrictions. The Chinese economy has expanded from that point. Then in 1991, India began to open its economy to international trade and entrepreneurial investment. In 1989, the Cold War ended with the fall of the Berlin Wall. Representative governments erupted in Eastern Europe and even Russia. Potentially more than 2 billion people in Asia and Eastern Europe were added to the open economies of the West.

Meanwhile, the U.S. economy went through waves of reorganization in the 1980s and again in the 1990s, driven by the expansion of Internet communications and new industries based on information and brainpower. The Internet continues to evolve and expand everywhere. Its particular relevance to international trade and Southern California is that it dramatically reduced the cost and greatly increased the speed of communications, allowing companies and individuals to operate easily worldwide. Larry Keller, former managing director of the Port of Los Angeles, told me in 2006 that until Internet communications became widespread in the late 1990s, the port had "empty terminals looking for tenants." Then "space tightened up," Keller recalled, as trade expansion accelerated.[7]

Toys Are Global

The story of Charles Woo illustrates the equations of trade and shared international production. Woo is the founder of Megatoys Inc., a Los Angeles firm that spawned a regional industry (see Figure 1.3).[8] With

Figure 1.3. Charles Woo and brother Peter Woo, founder and chief operating officer of Megatoys Inc., leaders of Los Angeles' emergent toy industry. Photo by Christine Carter Conway.

a master's degree in physics from his native Hong Kong, Woo came to the United States in 1978 to study for a doctorate in physics at UCLA. His family later joined him. But he quickly decided not to press on for the doctorate because he was impatient to found a business. He wanted to rescue his parents and brother from working long hours at their restaurant in Redondo Beach, a seaside community in Los Angeles County. "Moving papers is better than moving food," Woo remarked with a slight smile when he and I talked in 1995, the first of many conversations over the years. He is a wryly humorous but straightforward man, his speech as unadorned as the no-frills warehouse of Megatoys, where he greets visitors in a conference room and office just off the shipping dock floor. In 1980, Woo leased this warehouse in a skid row area near downtown Los Angeles and started importing toys made in China and shipped from Hong Kong. Then he tried to obtain orders from retail stores and chains. But instead of a conventional importing and distribution operation, Woo sparked a new pattern of business when immigrants who worked at menial jobs in restaurants and factories in the Los Angeles area asked him for toys on consignment so they could sell them at weekend swap meets, the supermarkets of the immigrant poor.

Sales were brisk. And as the consignees sold toys, they asked Woo for more and he had to expand his warehouse space to accommodate them. But as business grew, Woo also altered the traditional patterns of importing. "In the early days, I was just a middleman, receiving goods and sending them on," he recalls. There was scant profit in that, however. So he and his brother Peter, who joined Charlie in Megatoys, reached out to toy designers in the Los Angeles area who have created creatures and props for the movies since the original Mickey Mouse. Southern California remains a world-leading location for toy and animation designers, thanks to the need in the past half century for imaginative theme park attractions and for video game animation.

The Woos began to have toys designed in Southern California and then sent designs and product specifications by Internet to manufacturers in China. They monitored the output for quality control, oversaw every stage of shipment and customs clearance, and received the goods at the ports of Los Angeles and Long Beach. From there they shipped the toys to retail distribution centers in the United States and Mexico. Megatoys thus became more than a peddler of small plastic toys—cars, dolls, and coloring slates. It became a business that combined Southern California concepts with manufacturing in China and shipment back to the United States. "We design here, to take advantage of Hollywood ideas for toys and games," explains Charlie Woo. "We need the newest designs because the profit cycle is so short—you can't sit on a product for three or four months."

One result of the shift to design and product origination was a rapid growth in the company's sales and profit. Doing the brainwork behind the toys gave Megatoys the lion's share of profits in the trans-Pacific process. "Foreign" trade thus became a collaborative endeavor, not a middleman business. Today, Megatoys is close to $100 million in annual sales and employs two hundred to four hundred people depending on the season. Peter Woo explains the economic value process by citing the premier coffee chain. "It's like Starbucks," he says. "They don't grow the coffee beans but they get most of the money that customers pay for the cappuccinos." Stated another way, global production systems—"supply chains"—are not new things in the world. But modern communications, the Internet and related technologies, have changed many of the relationships between designer and manufacturer, importer and exporter.

Meanwhile, the Woos' enterprise became an inspiration for a new Southern California industry that today boasts more than one thousand companies designing, importing, and distributing more than $10 billion of toys annually across the United States and into Mexico and Canada. Los Angeles has surpassed New York as the chief center for toy distribution in the United States.[9] Geographic location has a lot to do with that. Local companies can get toys from China into a customer's hands anywhere in the United States in two weeks, whereas it would take a month for goods to move to East Coast ports and accomplish the same delivery.

Toys come mainly from China and buyers come from everywhere. "We sell to companies that have truck stops across America," says May Fong, who runs a small outlet for Tai Tung Co. in a warren of streets near Los Angeles City Hall. What do truck stops buy? "What drivers buy for their children, trucks and dolls," Fong says. Meanwhile, A&A Plush Toys, a Korean-owned company in Carson, has buyers from Argentina ordering stuffed animal merchandise that is made in Qingdao, China, for a Seoul toy firm that ships the products to Southern California for distribution to Latin America.

The toy industry took a hit in 2007 when it was discovered that Chinese manufacturers had used lead paint in some toys. U.S. companies recalled hundreds of thousands of toys; a Chinese toymaker in Guangdong committed suicide because of the disgrace. Ultimately, U.S. and Chinese companies instituted new procedures. Global recession, however, held down toy imports again in 2008.

Of course, Southern California has had a toy industry for decades. Mattel, the company that gave the world the Barbie doll in 1959, Hot Wheels in the 1960s, and several other standards, was founded in 1945. The company was a huge success at a time when Los Angeles became renowned for creativity and fashion, whether in clothing, television entertainment, political influence, or lifestyles. Mattel even prefigured the global economy by gathering components for Barbie from more than a half-dozen countries. The doll was manufactured of ethylene produced in Taiwan from oil produced in Saudi Arabia, but she had nylon hair from Japan and clothing from Italy, along with other parts from Malaysia. Barbie ultimately was assembled in China and shipped from Hong Kong to Mattel in the Los Angeles area or to 140 other countries where she was sold. Mattel thus originated "supply chain management," bringing parts from all over the world together with precise timing and economy. It was a singular feat decades ago but these days is simply routine for thousands of companies, many of them far smaller than Mattel, which now has almost $6 billion in annual revenues and employs thirty thousand people in forty-three countries.[10]

Archipelago of Companies

By contrast, the contemporary industry in Southern California, represented by the Woos' Megatoys, is even more remarkable: an archipelago of small companies and individuals working in concert with worldwide suppliers and customers. The operations of this archipelago can work in a decentralized system because communications via Internet, satellite, cellular transmission, and other forms are now highly developed and inexpensive. financing also is available today for all the small and medium-sized companies that comprise this industry. And no wonder—it's a big market. The small company toy industry of this region generates, at a conservative estimate, $10 billion in annual revenues and employs twenty-five thousand people.

The new international industries of Southern California involve far more than toys, of course. The example of Jennie Kiang, an immigrant from Taiwan, and her relationship with giant Wal-Mart Stores illustrates one aspect of the way Southern California, and the whole U.S. economy, makes its living through the exchange of information and ideas—not to mention goods and services—with other countries. Kiang and her husband Raymond founded HYI in 1979 as an importer of shoes, which a Taiwanese relative supplied from a manufacturing plant in mainland China, then in the early days of opening trade in response to Deng Xiaoping's liberalization policies.[11]

Like Charlie Woo, Kiang started out as a simple importer: "you imported shoes, shipped them to the customer, and got paid," she recalled in 2001. But her business expanded greatly and got a lot more complicated when she attracted a big customer, Wal-Mart, which gave her orders for hundreds of thousands of hiking boots, golf shoes, and other footwear. Wal-Mart took Kiang's HYI to new heights—the firm today does close to $17 million in annual sales to a broad selection of retailers of footwear for hiking and golf, hunting and fishing. But with growth has come much more responsibility. "Wal-Mart wants us to do marketing and product planning and inventory control for them," Kiang says. So her firm now employs sixty people at its headquarters in Covina, including senior managers who must make decisions on which models of hiking boots and athletic shoes need special sales promotions. And HYI must keep up with changing tastes in boots and shoes through its own style consultant, who does market research at gatherings of young people.

Instructions on new fashions and orders for more shoes are beamed to HYI's agents, who are based in Guangzhou, China. They order the shoes, monitor the quality, and provide the necessary information about the products and the factories that produced them to U.S. customs agents, who are on-site in China. They then arrange for shipments to the ports of Long Beach and Los Angeles. At that point, HYI employees break down shipments, directing specific quantities to distribution centers across the United States. This system is only made possible by extraordinary information processing and communication. But it is certainly not unique. Rather, Kiang's HYI exemplifies the global supply chain that brings most products to the U.S. retail system from China or Latin America.

To be sure, the numbers seem to show that America is buying much more than it is selling overseas these days. U.S. imports, at $2.3 trillion in 2007, were more than 40 percent larger than U.S. exports, at $1.6 trillion. China, which exports $256 billion a year more than it imports from the United States, is the target of criticism and threats by the U.S. Congress to impose tariffs and restrictions on Chinese exports. But the statistics are misleading because they have not kept up with the reality of international trade. The products on sale in the United States today, whether a dress bought at Target or a Dell computer ordered online, are decidedly American in economic content and value even though they may have been made overseas. This is not the stuff of deficit but of the enlarged landscape of global industry, designed as it is to serve the highly developed U.S. economy.

Typically, on dolls, boots, computer parts, and other merchandise, China gets one-fifth or less of the product's value although import figures credit it with more. The accounting swells the trade deficit with China and leads to disputes about trade. China protests that the "trade deficit" is much overstated, yet the U.S. Department of Commerce has not yet altered its methods of record keeping. Businesspeople know better. "The trade deficit figures are totally bogus," said Dominic Ng, chairman of East West Bank, based in Pasadena, and a director of Mattel.[12] "Imports coming here might be from Hungary and Malaysia with some assembly done in China before shipping to America. But to say on that account that China is one-third of the U.S. trade deficit makes no sense." The truth is that most of the value is reaped by the creator, designer, and marketer of the product, as we see in the products that Megatoys or HYI or indeed Mattel designs but has manufactured in China. Put another way, Mattel makes more profit from Barbie than any low-cost manufacturer because it created Barbie and owns the brand—the intellectual property of the doll—and built the wholesale and retail market for it.

Expert testimony to the U.S. Congress some years ago defined the value that China reaps from its exports. Economist Lawrence J. Lau, vice chancellor of the Chinese University of Hong Kong and former economics professor at Stanford University, explained the concept in 2003 to a hearing of the U.S. Congressional-Executive Commission on China. "Precisely because Chinese firms are mostly engaged in assembly/finishing operations, the domestic value-added content of Chinese exports to the U.S. is low," Lau told members of Congress. "It may be estimated at 20 percent" of the value of the product to the company that owns it and sells it on the retail market, he said.[13] Indeed, the Chinese themselves don't believe they're getting 20 percent of that value. "We get 10 percent of the value of the products, because we only manufacture," says Sufeng Yao, chief of the commercial office at the Chinese consulate in Los Angeles.[14] That's why Chinese businesspeople are seeking to form partnerships with companies in Southern

California—to own more parts of the supply chain. Another aim is to establish a brand name for Chinese goods that will allow them to command a higher price and profit margin.

Moving Markets

It's important that we understand these shifting equations and relationships because international trade is an evolving video game, not a still picture. Inevitably, China and India, like South Korea before them, will become more than suppliers of cheap goods. They will compete for business at all levels, own companies in the United States, and partner with them in Asia and around the world. Indeed, this is already happening. In 2008, an Indian company, Vedanta Resources PLC, purchased Asarco LLC, a more than one-hundred-year-old copper mining company in Arizona. More than five hundred Chinese companies now have offices or operations in Southern California. They want to set up operations or work with American companies to increase their share of the proceeds from trade between China and the United States. "Chinese companies want to move up the value chain. They see increasing their part in distribution and marketing as ways to accomplish that," says Stacy Sun, a business consultant in Los Angeles who organized a two-day conference in July 2007 that drew forty-five Chinese companies and three hundred U.S. firms interested in joint ventures.[15]

Puluosi Lighting of Changzhou, China, and its American division, Plus Lighting of La Verne, California, illustrate the trend. The Puluosi factory in Changzhou, a city of 3.5 million on the Yangtze River, makes halogen lamps to light streets and parking lots. It makes many of its lights on contract for General Electric, Philips, and Sylvania, says Daniel Qian, president of Plus Lighting. Business has been good, and sales in the United States grew to $10 million a year. But three years ago, Puluosi made a move for more, investing $2.5 million in the La Verne complex to assemble its own lamps, to be branded as Plus Lighting. Qian says he is trying to market more of the Plus brand. Why? "Because of the profit margins," he explains. On equipment for other lighting suppliers, "we make 20 percent to 30 percent profit margin, but on our own brand name, we can make 60 percent to 70 percent." He is seeking an American partner to help distribute the Plus brand name.

It's a story that might be disturbing to many Americans who fear that the United States is losing its industrial abilities; as the saying goes, "we don't make anything in America anymore." Yet the record shows U.S. industry broadly to be adaptive and innovative in the age of globalization. For example, the apparel industry remains a vibrant industry in Southern California—comprising 11,500 companies with 122,000 employees—despite years of competition from production in low-wage countries, including China. Adaptation can be through fashion and specialization. George Rudes, a veteran apparel manufacturer, came up with a way to produce moderately priced fashion that overcomes competition with cheap merchandise. "China can land a blue jean in Los Angeles for $8.50," said Rudes, who at age seventy-eight has spent sixty years in the apparel trade. "You can't compete directly with that," he told me in 2006. "But if you have a specialty or a fashion, you can win." He did just that by founding a company in 2005 with his daughter Lisa to make reinforced "Tummy Tuck" jeans for women in their middle years. They named the firm Not Your Daughter's Jeans, and the denim jean, with a mesh-reinforced abdominal panel and flexible stretch fabric in the thighs, has been a huge success, now passing $55 million in annual sales. The jeans sell at retail for $80 a pair, which is moderate department store pricing, and yet, Rudes says, the jeans are "all made here, except for the fabric. For fabric though, I have to supply from China because that's where denim is made now."[16]

The old image of the apparel industry is of sweatshops. But in today's Southern California business, the computerized machinery is too expensive and demanding of skills to entrust to underpaid workers. For example, at Todd Rutkin, Inc., a company that uses massive computerized cutting machines to slice fabric precisely, operators of cutting machines make $15 per hour with health benefits, and employees trained in computerized pattern-making earn $50,000 a year. True enough, in the worldwide apparel industry, conditions frequently resemble Charles Dickens's worst depictions of the Industrial Revolution. But new U.S. trade legislation is imposing stricter criteria on labor conditions in supplier countries, which should lead to beneficial effects in those countries, whether in Central America or Asia.

Labor standards could rise as some California importers react to competition by organizing their own efficient supply chains. Henry Fan, for example, now is president of Basic Elements Inc., a company in Irwindale, in the San Gabriel Valley, that imports children's clothing for Toys "R" Us and women's fashions for Chico's and other stores. Risks are substantial in working with large volumes of apparel under contract with retail merchants, Fan explains: "If something goes wrong, you have to air-freight rather than ship to meet the schedule and your margin for error is very thin." So Fan, an immigrant from Taiwan who earned an accounting degree from the University of California at Berkeley and worked in software in Silicon Valley before coming to the apparel trade in Southern California, has bought a factory in China and acquired control of companies in the United States that need efficient deliveries of apparel. "With more control, I have an advantage," Fan says.[17] The point is that even in a timeworn industry like apparel, low-wage countries such as China can expand rather than diminish the overall business and create opportunities for local firms to adapt and thrive.

But more significant than playing defense to counter low prices of imported goods, Southern California companies can develop technology to open growing markets in Asia, where the rising standard of living is creating customers for traditional merchandise and new procedures alike. A prime example is Avery Dennison Corp., of Pasadena, a maker of labels and identification tags for products of every kind. Its traditional product lines are benefiting anew from changing customs overseas. "China now has American style drugstores selling lots of shampoo and personal care products," noted Philip Neal, a retired chairman of the company. As a result, "our electronically printed labels on plastic bottles for such products are a booming business for us." Asia, Eastern Europe, and Latin America are growth areas for the company, and it is boosting investment in China and India.[18]

In new technology, Avery Dennison sees opportunities in radio frequency identification, or RfiD, which relies on microscopic radio wave emitters and identification receivers that are built into each product. The technology increasingly will be used in stores such as Wal-Mart to easily identify products and in hospitals to securely identify medicines. The Department of Homeland Security also uses RfiD to check every container that comes across the ocean. "With RfiD, the company saw great potential for growth," said Dean Scarborough, the company's president, to the *Los Angeles Business Journal* in 2006. "What was needed in RfiD was a company that could manufacture as much product as possible for the lowest cost possible. When you think about it, it is exactly what Avery does in label materials, just higher tech. We couldn't afford to not establish ourselves as the leader in this market." It is also a local development, as basic technology for RfiD was invented at the California Institute of Technology, just a few blocks away from Avery Dennison headquarters. The company was a backer of Caltech's research and one of the first customers for the commercial RfiD product. Innovation and the enlarged international economy, particularly in China, have paid off for Avery Dennison, which has $5.6 billion in annual revenues. The company has expanded its employee rolls by one-third to thirty thousand in recent years, thanks in good measure to business in China, where Avery Dennison has opened a research center to collaborate with its home base in Pasadena.[19]

Logistics of the Physical Internet

A major example of Southern California industry benefiting from expanded trade and new technology is "logistics," an age-old but newly named business that combines transportation, warehousing, freight forwarding, and distribution in what the *Economist* magazine has called "the physical Internet." Logistics has grown to be a $900 billion national phenomenon, according to the Commerce Department. Globally, the logistics industry posts aggregate annual revenues of $3.4 trillion, according to a study by Michigan State University.[20] In Southern California, the industry has brought prosperity and hundreds of thousands of good jobs.

Weber Distribution, for example, is a more than eighty-year-old family-owned company that reflects the promise of the industry. The firm was a simple trucking operation located in burgeoning Los Angeles of the 1920s and 1930s and then a warehousing and trucking operation in the great post–World War II expansion in the area. Goods would be shipped to Los Angeles by rail or interstate highway, stored in Weber warehouses, and distributed around the region by Weber vehicles. "Eveready entrusted its batteries to us and we saw to it that they were shipped to retailers as needed," says Nicholas Weber, recently retired company president and grandson of the founder.[21] But in the 1990s the business changed with the growth of international shipments and even more with the growth of technology. Weber, with headquarters in Santa Fe Springs, southeast of the city of Los Angeles, is now "a total solutions provider," says Bill Butler, a son-in-law who stepped up to company president in 2007. He means that Weber gives clients who have goods made elsewhere constant information about the products, monitoring shipments all the way from the factories through customs clearance overseas and on ships coming across the Pacific and through the ports of Los Angeles to final delivery. "We give them the information they need to plan a month or more ahead in their marketing," Butler says. Doing all that takes sophisticated computing and communications systems; Weber's warehouses are monuments to information science, with goods on palettes stacked on shelves several stories high. The goods are tracked constantly by an information system that includes handheld personal digital assistants that have become the required tools for forklift operators.

Information costs money. In 1999, Nick Weber says, he made the decision to spend "hundreds of millions" on the necessary information systems. The company at that time had a division that concentrated on moving goods for the military. It was a good business, he recalls, "but we sold it in order to invest in the information system." Without that decision the company might have gone out of business because it would not have been able to adapt as the number of container shipments increased many times over in just this decade. "We handled fewer than two hundred containers a month in 2000," Butler says. "Today we handle twenty-five hundred containers a month." So the company has gone from six containers a day to more than one hundred a day. Back then it had two warehouses; today, it has eleven—seven in Southern California and the others stretching east to Las Vegas and Phoenix and north to the San Francisco Bay area. Trucks move twenty-four hours a day, six days a week. "And I remember times when if we did one container in a week, I'd go out and have a beer after work," Weber said.

But perhaps the most arresting aspect of Weber Distribution's story—and that of logistics—is that employment has increased with growth and so have pay scales. In six years, the company has more than doubled annual revenues to more than $100 million and increased the number of employees from fewer than two hundred to more than five hundred. And the pay is better. Warehousing jobs that paid minimum wage a generation ago are now better-paid skilled positions, for which there is an expanding demand. "The pay for a forklift operator is $13 an hour before benefits," reports Butler. To be sure, he concedes, there are operations in the region's vast beehive of warehousing and trucking that pay wages closer to $10 an hour to move goods. But Butler observes, "if you're in business to provide a service, you need employees who know how to use the technology—and there's a great demand for them."

As skills have upgraded, so have titles—and incomes. The traditional shipping clerk is now called a logistics specialist and commands $35,000 a year in pay. "More than that," says Peter Woo of Megatoys. "For a good shipping clerk you must pay $50,000 or more." As for people in the front offices, greater credentials are required. In the front office of Weber Distribution, for example, high school diplomas long ago were replaced by a demand for college degrees, and now, master's degrees in business administration and law degrees are common. Logistics has become a major industry, with U.S. railroads, truckers, and delivery service companies experiencing 15 percent growth in revenues and profits per year.

Trade with Mexico and Latin America is also growing as companies there see opportunity in the big market of El Norte. And that translates into another need for logistics support because many companies in Latin America don't have connections with warehousing and transport networks in the United States. So Marcelo Sada, an entrepreneur from Monterrey, Mexico, figured out a solution. He started a warehouse company named Source Logistics in 1999 in Montebello, in Southern California, to help Latin American companies, such as the Mexico City bakery Grupo Bimbo, distribute their food products to grocery firms in the United States. Source Logistics has been a success, growing to fifty employees and $7 million in annual revenues, as Latino populations have swelled and spread across the United States. Sada, a member of one of Mexico's leading business families, now imports products from Guatemala, Costa Rica, El Salvador, Colombia, Brazil, Peru, Argentina, and Mexico. Source has operations in Laredo and Galveston, Texas, and in Atlanta, to serve the expanding Latino market in the Southeast. "The strategy is simple," Sada says. "I open operations near ports of entry—San Diego, Los Angeles, Laredo—and in places of high Latino population." His next new territory is Chicago, which historically has had a large Latino workforce.[22]

Trade, logistics, and the continuing expansion of global markets all add up to great promise, says economist John Husing, of Redlands, California, an authority on the Inland Empire areas of San Bernardino and Riverside. "The rise of trade through our Southern California harbors has given our area its first competitive advantage for creating good-paying blue-collar jobs since the rise of aerospace in World War II." He predicts that 1 million new jobs will open up "to the 44 percent of local adults with no college experience," if the necessary investments are made in infrastructure of dedicated high-speed truck lanes and rail grade separations.[23]

Fortunately, the investments are already in the works. Legislation for bond financing of $20 billion to upgrade the state's highways and infrastructure received unanimous backing from political parties and strong approval from California voters in 2006. The $2.2 billion Clean Air Action Plan for the Los Angeles and Long Beach ports is also receiving strong support, as it must.[24] As great as traffic through the ports is today, it is nonetheless expected to double in the next twelve years. Voters would not allow such growth if air pollution from idling freighters and trucks were not curbed. Again fortunately, the record of the public agencies that own and operate the ports has been relatively good in adapting to change for more than one hundred years. And the current managements of those agencies are avowedly determined to continue that record by giving Southern California the most environmentally suitable ports in the world—a leadership position on a growing industry worldwide.

Knowledge as Product

Finally, we should understand that the most significant product for Southern California's place in the global economy is the output of knowledge industries like electronics and software. But it is in those industries, particularly, that production and research are shared between personnel here and in India and other countries. That process of shared knowledge has been derided as "outsourcing" and "offshoring." Many fearfully predict that outsourcing will send jobs flying over the ocean while college-educated Americans idle away their days in dead-end occupations or glum unemployment. In 2005, the Federal Reserve Bank of Dallas estimated that the number of jobs outsourced in fields ranging from art design to sales could climb from less than 1 million to 3.3 million in 2015. And prominent economist Alan Blinder of Princeton University said in a 2006 essay that as many as 40 million U.S. jobs in service industries could be "offshored" to India and other countries over the coming two decades or so.[25] Neither Blinder nor the Dallas Fed was merely scaremongering with the projections. Rather, they were arguing that the world economy is changing and that educated workers in India and other nations are capable of doing service industry jobs that Americans do now. Their call was for U.S. government and private policy makers to think about changing educational and social policies to meet changed circumstances.

To be sure, globalization is a massive and sometimes confusing affair. Many people believe that America is somehow weakened by the economic rise of other nations and by historic shifts from old jobs and industries to new ones in a wider economy. But there is more to celebrate than to fear in this new U.S. economy, and more to understand than to deny. Southern California has hosts of examples to demonstrate the positive shape of things to come. A look at three such examples shows, again, that shared knowledge is not a one-way street but a complex interchange. For understanding, we might look first at the San Diego area, where small companies share work on the leading edges of telecommunications technology with partners in India and China and other countries.

P. J. Go, a founder and former president of Continuous Computing Corp., a San Diego firm that makes software systems for cell phones, says that demand is tremendous for added capability—for what is termed 3G, or third-generation cell phone applications. "What we have to keep in mind is that telephone density in India [the number of people with access to telephone communications] is 13 percent of the 1 billion population," Go said in an interview. "In China, it is 42 percent of 1.3 billion people—in the U.S. it would be over 90 percent. Cellular companies want to greatly increase the applications customers can access by cell phones so they can attract new subscribers." Work on the necessary electronics and software to achieve cellular advances goes on twenty-four hours a day at Continuous Computing. But not all the work is done in San Diego. More than half of the company's four hundred employees are overseas.[26]

"We serve India and China and have 90 people in India and 120 in China," but the people do somewhat different work, says Go, who came to California from Cebu City in the Philippines to study electrical engineering at Occidental College in Los Angeles and then at the California Institute of Technology in Pasadena. "Architecture of the software and marketing is done here in San Diego, but implementation is done in China and India," he says. That doesn't mean "merely low-level implementation," he explains; "employees everywhere are involved in generating ideas." "People work together, sharing information, and that makes the business possible," Go adds. He has moved on to be general manager of Adlink Technology America, an information company in Irvine. Continuous Computing, which is backed by a half-dozen major venture capital investors, including Intel Corp., has customers among major electronics and computer companies in Japan, Korea, India, China, Germany, France, Sweden, and throughout Europe. It also serves sixteen major U.S. companies, including IBM and Hewlett-Packard. The point for Continuous Computing and many other U.S. companies is that jobs are not moving out but are being created because larger markets are expanding the business. In a new era of sharing work, the relevant question to ask is: Would we have the work if we did not have the sharing?

For an answer we may consider Conexant Systems, a Newport Beach company with an impressive legacy as a division of Rockwell International, where under a Defense Department contract it invented the computer modem for communicating data over telephone lines. That inventive division became independent in 1999 as Conexant and succeeded as a producer of the intricate microchip brains behind Internet access for home computers and set-top boxes that connect televisions to satellite transponders. But in that growing field, Conexant has many competitors worldwide, and so Dwight Decker, who retired this year as chief executive but remains chairman, moved half of his engineering work to India in 2005.

Conexant now employs seven hundred engineers in Orange County, California, and about nine hundred at work in Hyderabad, India. Engineers in India make the rough equivalent of $25,000 a year compared with about $100,000 a year for comparable engineers in California. Architecture of the complex semiconductors is largely done in California, as is conceptualizing of future products in consultation with customers. But the chips and software are produced in India. That means, Decker told me in 2005, "I can get more engineers working for less cost and so develop new products faster and succeed." Decker explained that Conexant's work represents a phase in the global economy's development. The sophisticated microchips the firm produces find customers among the advanced economies, such as Japan and South Korea—where Samsung Electronics is a big customer—as well as the United States and Europe. India is not yet at a stage where it is a big market for Internet protocol TV and other advanced products, but it will become a giant market in the future. Decker, who has a Ph.D. in mathematics from Caltech, is optimistic. He sees opportunities for companies like Conexant as India moves up the value chain. The United States still leads in information technology, he says, and "we can sustain our world leadership if we continue to innovate." Clearly, however, competition is and will be constant.[27]

Adam Bartkowski, founder and former president of Apriso Corp., offers a similar perspective. The company, based in Long Beach, produces software called FlexNet that governs and monitors all aspects of modern production, maintenance, warehousing, and use of labor. It is a complex product that costs up to $1 million a copy, and it has found customers in thirty-nine countries. To Bartkowski, that success confirms the vision for the U.S. and world economy that led him to found Apriso in 1999 with backing from venture capital in Southern California. America, Bartkowski says, is now "the creator, the framework architecture economy," that determines what goods and services are produced everywhere.[28]

The world economy has seen such leadership before, says Bartkowski, who immigrated to the United States from Poland as a child and later earned degrees in mathematics from the Massachusetts Institute of Technology and in business from Northwestern University. He cites imperial Britain in the nineteenth century as an earlier "framework architect," and further back, before the economic rise of Europe, China played a similar role. Today, the United States is playing the leadership role because the size of its gross national product at $14 trillion is greater than the combined GNPs of the next six economies.[29] China and India, at $3.2 billion and $1 billion, respectively, in annual output, face decades of development to create complex consumer economies. Right now, they are beginning that long process with the collaboration of the United States. The opportunities for the leading economy today are unprecedented, Bartkowski says. "five billion people are connected in the world economy—83 percent of the world's population—and that makes the world a much bigger pie."

Being framework architects doesn't mean that Americans make everything, or even think up everything, Bartkowski argues. It means they have a central role to play in activities worldwide. If bright people in other countries and continents have ideas, they should be welcomed because new ideas increase the market for all ideas and expand the world economy. Indeed, Bartkowski reached out to his native Poland to have some of its software developed in Krakow as he was building Apriso, which now manages five hundred FlexNet installations worldwide. "If we tried only to do America business we would have no business," Bartkowski says succinctly. "Don't be afraid of the bigger pie."

Clearly, these examples show Southern California businesses to be involved in world-changing trends and events. Yet almost none of the companies I've cited are of enormous corporate size. They are relatively small and entrepreneurial but nonetheless capable of attracting financing and investment. A lot of investment is flowing into Southern California these days, from across the United States and around the world. Those related facts speak to new and different structures in this region's economy that make it a model for others. The next two chapters will explain the shifts in technology and in finance that have supported innovative small companies and helped bring about the changing global economy.

Ballistic Missiles to Cellular Phones

The Shift in Southern California's
Industrial Foundation

> The broadband revolution truly is of the same magnitude as
> the industrial revolution of the 1800s.
>
> Henry Samueli,
> Broadcom Corp., cofounder and chairman

SOUTHERN CALIFORNIA was one of the pioneers of
the technology evolution and financial revolution that
have transformed the world economy over the past two decades. The
strength and promise of the region's economy today stem from these
achievements: the creation of the nascent Internet at UCLA and three
other institutions[1] and the changes in capital markets that allowed more
than half a million small to medium-sized companies in Southern California to raise money, survive, and thrive.[2]

This chapter focuses on the scientific and technological evolution
that took this region from an economy based on military and space
programs, funded by the federal government, to today's information-
based global industries, financed by private and public investments. The
change was historic—and unanticipated. Southern California's economy
had expanded with only slight pauses from the 1940s almost to the end
of the 1980s, first as the airplane-building arsenal of democracy during
World War II and then as the rocketry and spacecraft pioneering center
of the military-industrial complex. Its suburban prosperity was heavily
dependent on federal government contract work that employed more
than 1 million people in giant companies, such as Lockheed Aircraft,

North American Aviation, and Douglas Aircraft. Jobs in the aerospace-defense industry paid well. In the 1980s, pay for an industrial worker was $18 an hour—the equivalent of more than $30 an hour today—with full medical and pension benefits.

But when the Cold War ended in 1989–90 with the implosion of the Soviet Union and reductions in defense company contracts, the local aerospace-defense industry lost at least five hundred thousand jobs. The industry, which in the 1980s had accounted for more than $200 billion in annual revenues—and paychecks—shrank to a third that size.[3] Prospects were bleak. Many worried that the region's economy might never recover. Presidential candidate Bill Clinton, in a visit to the *Los Angeles Times* in August 1992, caught the general mood when he said in elegiac tones: "California was the place of unbridled opportunity for so long" because a national economic strategy based on defense and space had given the state a "high wage, high growth economy." Now that day was over, Clinton said, and there was no clear national strategy for replacing defense as an economic engine.[4]

Author Joan Didion, a native Californian, saw cultural decline in both the defense industry's largesse and its downturn. In a 1993 essay in the *New Yorker* magazine that became a central part of her book *Where I Was From*, she wrote that in decades of defense industry boom, great flows of "other people's money" had eroded the old pioneering culture of California and allowed people to think that prosperity came easily. The future, as she saw it in 1993, would hold decidedly less opportunity. She wrote that economists promising "a workforce more inclined toward entrepreneurship" meant, "in other words, no benefits and no fixed salary, a recipe for motel people."[5] That was Didion's characterization of people too poor to qualify for a long-term rental, much less a mortgage on a house.

More Opportunity

Yet the opposite happened—renewal not decline—because key sectors of today's information-based economy emerged from the defense industry's core of scientific research and technological development. Entrepreneurship meant *more* opportunity. California companies led a national trend in the 1990s toward more emphasis on innovation and job creation in independent, small and medium-sized companies rather than large corporations. That trend has proved durable. According to the Census Bureau's *Statistical Abstract,* there are more than 27 million small business establishments in the United States today, comprising 7.2 million companies with fewer than one hundred employees plus 20.6 million self-employed businesses. The total is up from 21 million in 1990. Almost 4 million of those small businesses, 15 percent of the total, are in California, which has more small companies than any other state (Texas is second). The biggest change in those numbers has been a 39 percent growth in the number of self-employed individual businesses.[6]

The spirit of enterprise allowed California to come all the way back from its doldrums of the early 1990s. Today, the state has more jobs in technology than it had at the peak of aerospace defense work in the 1980s—948,000 technology workers then, 1.03 million today. Internet and computer services, scientific and technical research and design have more than taken up the slack left by the retreat of aerospace. Indeed, the whole Southern California region expanded dramatically. The current recession has hit parts of the region hard; unemployment is above the national avereage. But still the prospect is that Southern California's population will grow to more than 30 million in the next four decades.[7]

How did all this happen? By a renewal of the entrepreneurial traits that had built the aerospace industry in the first place. Southern California's aviation pioneers, Allan and Malcolm Loughead (founders of Lockheed), Glenn Martin, Donald Douglas, Jack Northrop, and others, had designed and built some of the first airplanes, from the 1910s through the 1930s. The companies they founded manufactured fighters and bombers during World War II. After the war, they continued to produce advanced aircraft and also increasingly complex electronic systems under guidance and financing from the newly organized Department of Defense and the U.S. Air Force. But it was two smaller companies, Hughes Aircraft and Electronics and Ramo-Wooldridge, which later became TRW, that were particularly significant in the invention of satellite and wireless communications during the 1950s.

Howard Hughes, the visionary billionaire, had founded Hughes Aircraft in 1932 to support his interest in flying. During World War II, the firm worked on radio communications systems and reconnaissance aircraft. Research in those technologically advanced areas, including rocketry and orbiting satellites, attracted great engineers and scientists to Hughes after the war. Simon Ramo was among those who joined the firm in 1946. Then thirty-three years old, Ramo was already a renowned engineer who had earned dual doctorates at the California Institute of Technology and led the invention of the electron microscope at General Electric. At Hughes, he oversaw programs that integrated radar with wing-gun controls and air-to-air missiles. Such activities, because they required new forms of radar, signal tracking, and systems to guide missiles from earth, ultimately led to advances in computing and communications technology.[8]

Ramo described military needs that gave rise to civilian products and systems in his 1988 book *The Business of Science*, in which he recalled the ideas that bubbled up during his 1956 work on intercontinental ballistic missiles (ICBMs). "A satellite could be designed to serve as a communications relay," he wrote. Then with radio signals sent up to a receiver in the satellite and a transmitter directing the signal back down to earth, "a high satellite could put any two places on the planet in direct communications. . . . It would become practical to broadcast radio and TV programs intercontinentally and to send industrial, financial, medical and every other kind of data all over the globe."[9]

Howard Hughes, however, grew increasingly eccentric, to the point that Ramo and other engineers left his company. Ramo recalls in his book that when he and Dean Wooldridge, a Caltech associate and brilliant engineer, wanted to found their own company, Hughes was mystified. In several meetings with Hughes, Ramo and Wooldridge tried to explain to the billionaire that they were unwilling to work for an owner who never communicated with them and made peremptory decisions, such as ordering operations to move to Las Vegas. "We said that our people would not move to Las Vegas," Ramo said. But Hughes responded that he found it "strange to build an organization around the idea of democracy." Hughes, who had inherited his father's oil drilling tool company, did not understand a new era of entrepreneurial ownership and independent-minded skilled employees. But the Pentagon did. Right after Ramo and Wooldridge left Hughes Aircraft in 1953, the Defense Department forced Hughes to give up an active role in his companies and to install professional management. The government's action turned out to be productive. Hughes Aircraft went on to develop, among other breakthroughs, orbiting communications satellites for the military and ultimately for the worldwide commercial satellite systems we know today.

The Pentagon also gave the Ramo-Wooldridge team substantial contracts immediately. One of the company's first assignments was to work on an ICBM, which a Ramo-led team brought in successfully in four years. The company developed advanced communications technology for the Defense Department and the National Aeronautics and Space Administration (NASA), including the Pioneer deep space probes that sent signals back to earth for more than twenty years. It also devised semiconductors made from gallium arsenide, which allow faster electronic performance than silicon-based chips and therefore became a leading technology in the creation of cellular telephony. "We have always had a lot of good technology in this company," Ramo told me in 2000. "If we had developed it all ourselves we would have had to become a very large company."

Instead of growing into a very large company, however, Ramo-Wooldridge in 1958 merged with Thompson Products, an auto supply firm in Cleveland, to become TRW. It was a deal that spoke volumes about the commercial status of entrepreneurial companies at that time. Bankers and investment markets wouldn't back two individuals like Ramo and Wooldridge, no matter how bright and successful they were. financial markets wanted collateral. So Ramo's company merged, as he explained, to gain size and a public stock: "In those days, a company needed the stability of big revenues and paying a dividend. There was less capital available." TRW didn't falter. It went on to develop technology, backed by government funding and its own and Thompson's profitability, at Space Park, its one-hundred-acre campuslike headquarters in Redondo Beach. When the place was built in the late 1950s, Ramo asked the architect to design buildings with windows all around so that engineers could look at views and sculptures and "think up big things." Thus, Ramo pioneered workplace "campuses" for high-tech industry, an idea later identified with Silicon Valley in northern California. TRW also was a progenitor of many companies as its high-tech engineers went on to found their own firms throughout Southern California.

Sputnik Surprise

Meanwhile, in 1958, the year TRW was born, significant changes occurred in the Defense Department amid widespread anxiety in America
about a "missile gap." The Soviet Union launched Sputnik in 1957 and
caused concern that U.S. technological leadership was threatened. The
Defense Department organized an effort to invest in research called the
Advanced Research Projects Agency, or ARPA (sometimes referred to
as DARPA). As Stephen Segaller explains in *Nerds: A Brief History of the
Internet*, "ARPA was created in response to Sputnik. Sputnik surprised
the nation and the world. Eisenhower told the secretary of defense, 'I
don't want to be surprised like this again.' So they wanted an agency
created to fund especially promising high technology."[10] In ARPA's first
year, for example, it backed research in integrated circuits that became
a foundation of modern electronics.

In a move that ultimately changed the world profoundly, the agency
funded the creation of the ARPANET, based on ideas conceived by Paul
Baran, an engineer at RAND Corp., a think tank in Santa Monica that
performed advanced research for the Defense Department, particularly
the Air Force. As the Soviet Union and the United States faced each
other in the 1960s with ICBMs that could deliver terrible destruction
in one attack, Baran wanted a network that could survive a first nuclear
strike on the Pentagon's communications system. Such a system could
assure the ability to deliver a retaliatory strike on an adversary. What
was needed was a distributed system, not merely a decentralized system
with several command centers and many outposts but a structure that
was in essence all outposts and no command center. In a 1964 RAND
study called "On Distributed Communications," Baran suggested a
technology called "packet switching" that would allow a message on
a network to find its destination via any route available. ARPA liked
the idea because it was already looking for a way to share information
among the many research institutions it supported.

As a result, an effort began that brought together four computer
scientists, Lawrence Roberts, Robert Kahn, Leonard Kleinrock, and
Vinton Cerf, on a Pentagon project awarded in 1968 to UCLA, which
was connected to the Stanford Research Institute, UC Santa Barbara,
and the University of Utah. The project succeeded by 1969 in allowing

institutions to transfer files between computers and to work simultaneously from different locations on shared research projects. The ARPANET was born and progressed during the next two decades, through innovations from many centers in the United States and Europe, to become the Internet that today is at the center of the world economy.

Other notable Pentagon and NASA-backed research going on in Southern California at the time included work at the Jet Propulsion Laboratory and UCLA on ways to improve reception of signals from outer space or across battlefields where solar "noise" and jamming were prevalent. Over more than two decades, that research led to the development of cellular telephony and the wireless communications industry.[11] The long postwar period thus provided shining examples of civilian industries emerging from research undertaken for the military and space exploration—swords evolving into digital plowshares.

Yet when defense budgets started to decline in 1989, almost no one in Southern California thought such an evolution possible. Some analysts and venture capital investors in northern California were more attuned to the connection between aerospace defense work and the needs of the new economy. Michael Moritz, of Sequoia Capital, a leading venture firm in Palo Alto, understood. There is a lot of demand for "skills in telecommunications and imaging and advanced semiconductors," Moritz told me in 1989. "We're eager to listen and talk to people in aerospace about ideas, or even better about setting up a business."[12]

Moritz's judgment proved correct, of course. Engineers who worked at firms like TRW and Hughes became entrepreneurs in electronics and communications. For example, Henry Samueli, who later founded Broadcom Corp., worked on broadband Internet communications systems for the military at TRW from 1980 to 1985, after earning a doctorate at UCLA. "That was probably the best five years of experience I could have gotten," Samueli told me in 2006. "It changed my whole direction." In 1985, he returned to UCLA to teach electrical engineering, where he supervised research into ways of transmitting digital signals through microwave networks—the field universally called wireless today.[13]

While teaching at UCLA, Samueli joined several former TRW researchers who founded PairGain Technologies, a company that helped telephone companies offer broadband Internet access to customers who in the late 1980s were turning increasingly to home computing. The Internet connections in those days were provided mostly by cable companies that had connections to homes for television service; large telephone companies had not yet perfected their digital subscriber line (DSL) service.

Broadband Revolution

The economics of broadband fascinated Samueli, who later described them in an article for the Institute of Electrical and Electronics Engineers titled "The Broadband Revolution."[14] The phone system was built for voice traffic, a narrow pathway with many distortions, while digital communications—breaking signals into component bits and then recomposing them into recognizable voice or data communications—is a far more complex task. Yet, Samueli said, costs of the latter are lower by orders of magnitude, at $30 a month for sending information in digital form on broadband waves compared with $1,000 a month for traditional phone lines. It was obvious that telephone companies would have to improve their technology to overcome such a gap. More importantly, Samueli recognized that such a cost differential between the old way and the new in telecommunications constituted a revolution. "The broadband revolution truly is of the same magnitude as the industrial revolution of the 1800s," Samueli wrote, looking back in 2000 at the first commercial decade of the Internet, cellular phones, and online commerce—technologies that had evolved from military and space research in the 1950s and 1960s.

Samueli took a direct hand in furthering that revolution by founding Broadcom in 1991, in collaboration with Henry Nicholas, a UCLA graduate student in electrical engineering. The company made semiconductors that converted television pictures to digital signals that could be transmitted via satellite and then reconverted to TV pictures. Broadcom was an instant success and has since adapted or invented every advance in wireless communication, supplying electronics for such consumer products as Apple Computer's iPod and cellular phones that routinely access the Internet.

Samueli, now fifty-four years old, is impressed with the increasing power of cell phones and the multitude of tasks they can perform—communicating, computing, photographing, data storing, and researching via the Internet. "I want Broadcom to be the leading supplier of electronic components for wireless devices," he says. That seems a reasonable ambition for a corporation as large as Broadcom, with six thousand employees and more than $4 billion in annual revenue. But Samueli's company today must spend $800 million a year on company and university research and devote three-quarters of its skilled employees to research and development work if it hopes to stay abreast of technology.

It is a new world in more ways than one. As Samueli declared, "for a long time, the Defense Department was responsible for a good portion of this country's technology, from integrated circuits through satellite communications." But for almost two decades, the defense budget has been far less prominent in backing technology. In its place, private venture capital and the stock market have become the sources of financing for developing advanced microchips, Internet communications, and cellular telephones.

In the old days, an award of a defense contract gave a company security in working with innovative concepts. The famed Bell Laboratories division of American Telephone & Telegraph (AT&T), which invented the transistor in 1947, was the corporate model for technology development. But now, competition is fiercer, technological change is faster, and keeping up is harder. Broadcom faces competition on many fronts, from firms like Texas Instruments and Qualcomm in microchips for cell phones and aspects of phone operating systems. Small firms, focused on winning a place in the sun with newer technology, can change the competitive picture overnight. Stock prices gyrate dramatically for high-tech companies like Broadcom. Samueli, however, says the stock price is only a distraction. "We don't rely on it. You run your business independent of the stock market," he says. "You fund your R&D and manage the business for the profits, not on a quarter-to-quarter basis but on a one-to-two-year product cycle. The stock price eventually should reward investors and employees." (Samueli took a leave of absence from Broadcom in 2008 pending resolution of a civil lawsuit against him and cofounder Henry Nicholas by the U.S. Securities and Exchange Commission relating to stock option practices for Broadcom employees.)

For all its risks, the new flexible environment is enabling the U.S. economy to adapt to a new age that is no longer stationary but mobile, no longer national but international. The wireless telephony or cell phone business is not a mere niche in global communications; it practically *is* global communications, says a supplier of software for mobile phones. In 2008, the number of cell phones in use worldwide was over 2 billion. And the numbers are growing exponentially, says Naser Partovi, head of SKY MobileMedia of San Diego, a young and growing company. "Cell phones, iPods and other wireless devices now outnumber PCs in the world," notes Partovi, an immigrant from Iran by way of Canada, where he was educated and broke into business with Northern Telecom. He predicts that "wireless is only going to become more powerful, with greater memory and capabilities," for communications and computing.[15]

The new industry was born from military research performed mainly in Los Angeles, but it is now centered importantly in San Diego. The careers of two extraordinary engineers, Andrew Viterbi and Irwin Jacobs, who pursued research in communications, developed basic technology, and founded companies, illustrate the evolution of wireless communication and the changes that have come over all U.S. industry. first, we will follow the story of Viterbi because his invention was fundamental to the existence of cellular telephony. Born into a Jewish family in Bergamo, Italy, in 1935, Viterbi came to the United States at age four with his parents because Mussolini's Italy, like so much of Continental Europe in the 1930s, was unsafe for Jewish people. The family settled in Boston but struggled economically as Viterbi's ophthalmologist father, Achille, had difficulty getting reestablished here. But Andrew won a scholarship to the Massachusetts Institute of Technology (MIT), worked part time to support himself, and earned bachelor's and master's degrees in electrical engineering.

After graduation in 1957, Viterbi was recruited to a communications group at the Jet Propulsion Laboratory (JPL) in Pasadena, a part of Caltech that serves NASA as a research facility. While at JPL, he earned a doctorate at the University of Southern California (USC)—the only school that would allow him to pursue graduate study while working full time. And with that credential, he left JPL to take a teaching post at UCLA, where he developed the Viterbi algorithm. This research was financed by grants from DARPA and NASA. The algorithm is a mathematical tool that can distinguish faint digital radio signals from surrounding noise by calculating probabilities, whether on a battlefield infected with enemy jamming or in outer space amid the radioactivity of solar explosions. Its early success in the 1960s was critical for the development of cell phones. Viterbi is retired now from day-to-day business but lectures at universities, invests in startup companies, and donates philanthropically. He donated $52 million to the engineering school at USC in 2004. Having experienced fifty years of scientific progress and economic change, he is an expert witness to both the era of government funding of research and the contemporary environment of venture financing, stock market pressure, and uncertainty. In 2006, I found him to be clear-eyed about money and technology. He sees the Pentagon's historic backing of research, for instance, as a byproduct of the post–World War II period that lasted longer than it might have. "World War II gave Americans the impression that science was useful," he says with a smile. "But, I think those R&D funds would have petered out in the late forties, were it not for the Cold War."[16]

Computer Use Expands

Viterbi is respectful of the legacy of Bell Labs, but not of the old giant AT&T. The contributions and the influence of Bell Labs "were outstanding," Viterbi recalls. "The transistor was invented there and modern communications system theory came from Bell Labs." But change had to come and AT&T had to go. "The ARPANET did not come out of Bell Labs," he notes. "And if it had, the AT&T monopoly might have stifled or suppressed it. There is no doubt that communications development was slowed down by the monopoly," he says. "Technology would have happened anyway, but might have come from other countries." Instead, AT&T fell to deregulation of the telephone industry, and Internet communication changed the world. Viterbi was on the faculty of UCLA in the 1960s when ARPANET was developed there. He remembers the time when the researchers discovered they could send messages over the decentralized computing system "and e-mail was born." In fact, a whole new world was born because computers had been undergoing a parallel evolution. In the 1940s and 1950s, government and large corporations were the only organizations capable of operating computers. Then the minicomputer was introduced and "affordability went from the large corporation to small companies and groups," Viterbi says. Use of the minicomputer spread through the academic world but did not enter the lives of the general population until the personal computer expanded usage everywhere in the late 1970s and 1980s. In a mere few decades wireless and Internet "technologies have become pervasive—the peasant in China is connected as is the phone lady in Bangladesh with a micro loan," Viterbi says. When I suggested to him that he is a founder of this new world, Viterbi replied, "it is not false modesty to say only that I was in the right place at the right time."

But the fact is that he helped shape this time and place. In 1969, when he was at UCLA, Viterbi and fellow UCLA professor Leonard Kleinrock teamed with Irwin Jacobs, who was then teaching at the University of California, San Diego (UCSD). Together, the three started a company named Linkabit to share the consulting work they were getting from the military and the space agency. The company succeeded immediately, expanding to twenty-five employees in a few years. Communications was its strength because of the extraordinary expertise of its founders and the great pace of development in wireless research in the 1970s. Linkabit, for example, won a contract in 1975 to build jam-resistant two-way radios for the Air Force's fleet of planes and ground stations. The technology it developed was the predecessor of today's wireless networks or Wi-fi modems in laptop computers. Such innovativeness fed on itself as Linkabit attracted a choice group of engineers. It is credited with being the breeding ground of thirty-five companies in the San Diego area today. In 1980, after a decade in existence, it attracted an acquisition price of $25 million from Microwave Associates Communications, or M/A-COM, a conglomerate located in Massachusetts. Jacobs and Viterbi, both of whom had left university teaching in the early 1970s to work full time at Linkabit, stayed with M/A-COM for five years. Kleinrock, who had remained at UCLA to work on the ARPANET, never worked full time at Linkabit.

In 1985, Jacobs and Viterbi, with five associates, founded Qualcomm Inc., partly with the grubstake that M/A-COM's buyout gave them. Jacobs, two years older than Viterbi, also studied at MIT, although he didn't start out there. The son of a taxi driver, insurance salesman, and seafood restaurant owner, Jacobs always had an avid interest in math and science. But a high school counselor advised him to study hotel management because there was "no future in science or technology." So he began his studies at Cornell University in hotel administration. But after his first year he switched to electrical engineering on a scholarship, then went to MIT on a scholarship and earned a master's degree and a doctorate in three years. He stayed at MIT seven years more as an assistant professor and coauthored a textbook, *Principles of Communication Engineering*, which is still in use. He moved to Southern California in 1966 to join the newly created electrical engineering program at UCSD.[17]

The beginning of Qualcomm marked a shift toward adapting technology for the civilian economy. The company received a contract from the Federal Communications Commission to develop a satellite communications system that would allow long-distance truckers to stay in constant contact with dispatchers via text messages. Qualcomm produced OmniTRACS, which today connects half a million trucks worldwide. The system, said Viterbi in 2006, "really launched Qualcomm. In just a few years, it became profitable and that financed the early days of CDMA wireless."[18]

Jacobs and Klein Gilhousen, another of Qualcomm's cofounders, were working with a wireless operating system called code division multiple access (CDMA), which allowed cell phone calls to be sent over multiple frequencies simultaneously, thereby maximizing the available bandwidth. It could do this because the code division system broke down phone calls into packets of information, sent them out, and rebuilt the message at the recipient's end—just the way the Internet operates. Rival systems, which divided communications by time or single frequencies, were outpaced. CDMA also offered clearer reception because it used the Viterbi algorithm to block interference. As Jacobs explained in 2005, the idea of pursuing CDMA came to Qualcomm because Hughes Electronics had asked the firm to examine new satellite systems and find ways to improve communications. The CDMA system filled that need, but larger success for the system was not assured. Other cell phone operating systems were already in use, particularly in Europe, when Qualcomm brought CDMA on the scene in the late 1980s. Jacobs had to fight to gain acceptance at that time and fought again in the late 1990s to combat an attempt by European cell phone manufacturers to have Qualcomm's CDMA shut out of the international telecommunications system. But the superiority of the CDMA system won it a place in Asia, starting with South Korea. Now, as cell phone technology ascends to new levels of capability and complexity, CDMA has become the indispensable technological core of the worldwide industry.

Yet Qualcomm might not have attained that technological leadership were it not for a decision Jacobs made in 1995 to focus the company's efforts. The company in its early years worked to perfect the CDMA system and had won commercial success for it in Asia by 1995. Qualcomm at that time was making every part of the system—the cell phones, the microchips that were their technological operating systems, and the cellular base stations and related infrastructure of the cell network. As Jacobs explained, "we could either focus on the manufacturing or on the chips and technology development, but it was hard to do both unless we were much larger. We decided to focus on the chips; we sold the manufacturing business to Kyocera here in San Diego, and the infrastructure to Ericsson."

Intellectual Assets

Qualcomm decided not to try for giant corporate size. It focused more narrowly on the intellectual property part of the business, whereby Qualcomm employees constantly renew and expand cell phone capabilities. Its approach was in marked contrast to former ages, when a company became a giant of industry by controlling as much as it could. For instance, Henry Ford, at one point, owned every part of the car-making process, from mining the iron and making the steel, to adding the chrome bumper on the finished product. International Business Machines (IBM) exerted control over the early stages of the computer industry. But Qualcomm epitomizes the new and global age, in which intellect and information are the critical assets, and one acquires the rest on a constantly changing world market.

The choice proved wise, and Qualcomm has become a prosperous and world-renowned company. As of late 2008, Qualcomm had thirteen thousand employees and over $10 billion in annual revenue. It is a good-sized but not a giant company, other than in the strength of its intellectual capital. In 2007, the company took in $3.1 billion in license fees for its patents on CDMA technology—35 percent of its total revenues—and it earned more than $2 billion in profit on intellectual property, well over half its total profit.[19] Clearly, concepts and information structures produce value today.

To be sure, this is a deceptively simple statement. Depending on intellectual property to earn one's bread presents many challenges in today's global world. The piracy of filmed and recorded content in the entertainment media industry comes immediately to mind. And the long-term threat of the assault on patents and copyrights in legal thinking is a continuing subject of argument in the courts and of study in university law departments. Patent challenges are facts of everyday business life to companies like Qualcomm, which are challenged on patents by competitors and licensees alike.

But mostly, having a leadership place in global intellectual property demands constant and heavy investment to renew and expand the technology. In 2007, Qualcomm spent $1.8 billion, 20 percent of every sales dollar, on research and development to support its technology, which has a broadening potential because the multifaceted CDMA system is the heart of the newest advance in worldwide cellular telephony, the so-called third generation, or 3G. "All third-generation cellular is going to CDMA, ensuring that the technology will grow substantially," Jacobs says. Indeed, Jacobs predicted in 2008 that mobile phones will replace credit cards because the user's financial records will be embedded in the phone's circuitry—with appropriate security software. And the same will be true of medical records, "so you will be able to have health management through the mobile phone, diabetes testing, cardiac monitoring and the like."[20]

Clearly, shifting technology is giving individuals more access to communications and knowledge than ever before. And with such technology have come equally important changes in the economics and finance of business—from centralized control by large institutions to widely distributed power to individuals and small companies. Qualcomm's early financing, for example, came from private individuals, including

Younes Nazarian, a prominent Iranian immigrant businessman in Los Angeles. The company issued public stock in 1991 at $16 a share, and QCOM became a leading growth stock during the 1990s. Its 1.6 million shares outstanding now have a total value of $76 billion, attesting to the company's continued leading position in wireless telecommunications. Qualcomm's financing pattern—origins in government grants, later reliance on private investment—characterizes many Southern California entrepreneurial companies.

There is another way in which modern entrepreneurial companies like Qualcomm differ significantly from the old "Organization Man" corporate models of the past: in employee compensation and incentives. Qualcomm offers all employees a 15 percent discount on purchases of its stock during specified periods each year. Also, stock options for skilled employees are a central and highly prized component of an employee's compensation. (Broadcom offers similar incentives.) Options to buy stock at a fixed price, while over time the market price rises, used to be reserved for the highest company executives. That is how the legendary Alfred P. Sloan, president of General Motors from the 1920s to the 1940s, envisioned marrying "the managers' interests to those of the owners." In recent decades the concept has broadened to include all key employees, and in some companies, all employees. Modern retirement plans, such as the 401(k) plans, are also tied to investments that usually involve the stock market. This new world of risk-based finance, which contrasts sharply with the lack of finance in the 1950s for Simon Ramo and Dean Wooldridge, has supported the rise of entrepreneurial industry.

An example is the infrastructure of technological supplier companies that now dot the hills and canyons near UCSD. Peregrine Semiconductor, founded in 1979 by the research director of a U.S. Navy laboratory, is typical. Peregrine developed radio frequency integrated circuits for military and space satellites and is still in that business. "Our chips are in 90 percent of military satellites," says James Cable, the company's current chief executive, who led microelectronics research at Hughes Electronics and TRW for twenty-five years before joining Peregrine in 1996. In the 1990s, Peregrine turned to adapting its powerful chip sets to commercial uses, including cellular telephones and the base stations that enable their transmissions—reducing the size of its chipboard areas by 75 percent. "As a result," Cable says, "we have been able to put chips in cell phones and in all the cellular base stations and in digital cable television transmitters and receivers—the Blackberries have our chips." Peregrine has grown to two hundred employees and $50 million in annual sales in the past few years as cell phone demand has exploded. Its main financing today comes from nine venture capital funds that have invested collectively $140 million.[21]

In a similar vein, Sequoia Communications, a San Diego firm with forty-eight employees, has developed a 3G wireless chipset that works with all of the different operating systems, from Europe's global system mobile (GSM) up to the more sophisticated CDMA. Sequoia is financed by $63 million in investment from Motorola and Nokia and four venture capital financiers. They are backing the company, says Sequoia's founder John Groe, who once developed radio circuits for the military at TRW, because "we have proved that our concept is valid, that we can make a device work in all these interfaces." Tens of millions invested for "concepts" and seemingly small technological advances attest to a risk-based and change-embracing economy that is unique to the United States and to California, in particular, says Viterbi. "Only in America," he exclaims, with wonder. "I don't think there is any other country that has the entrepreneurial drive of America. In fact, after fifty years of working in Massachusetts and the East Coast and then here, I don't think there is any place like California for the entrepreneurial drive, the willingness to take risks, to invest in risk."

The California state motto, Eureka, or "I have found it," was set in 1849 to refer specifically to gold rush prospecting or to the state's abundance, which the hell-bent gold rushers had come upon. The word hints at the kind of people Viterbi is referring to: chance-takers looking for a fortune in the gold rush; Civil War veterans looking to start anew; immigrants from China who came and stayed despite prejudicial laws; sons of refugees from pogroms and hatred who gambled on a new business called the movies; farmers driven from the 1930s Dust Bowl to plant new roots in a better place; black Americans from the then-segregated South who came to Los Angeles and within two generations rose to a leading place in the city's politics and government; soldiers and sailors who came during World War II and then came back after the war to work and raise families in sunshine and a fertile economy; immigrants from Latin America and Asia who came—and are coming still—seeking opportunity and respect in a society based on liberty in law.

Spurred by entrepreneurial vigor, California anticipated and reflected a fresh burst of development in the entire U.S. economy. In the quarter century to 2007, U.S. employment rose 47 percent, from 99 million to 146 million. The country's total output of goods and services more than doubled, from $6 trillion a year in 1990 to $14 trillion in 2007. America's economy now is larger than the next five national economies combined.[22]

Productivity Grows

What has happened? Information technology increased U.S. economic productivity, just as electricity and the internal combustion engine did in the nineteenth and twentieth centuries, respectively. America today is getting more output for the same or even less input—more bang for the buck, so to speak. This is very important because productivity gains are the essential force that allows living standards to rise. Moreover, productivity in the United States has been rising faster than it has in other economies, reported Ben Bernanke, chairman of the Federal Reserve Board, in 2006. "One leading explanation for the strong U.S. productivity growth is that labor markets in the United States tend to be more flexible and competitive, characteristics that have allowed the U.S. to realize greater economic benefits from new technologies," Bernanke said.[23]

To be sure, the transformation of the U.S. economy has not been met with universal acclaim. The plaintive cry is still heard from many that "people used to have jobs for life; work has changed." Change in the 1980s, whether from Japanese competition or financial restructuring, often produced fearful prediction and outright condemnation. The rise in entrepreneurship in some minds has been more than offset by the decline of unions; the membership of organized labor has declined from 18 million workers and 24 percent of the labor force in 1973 to 15.7 million and 12.1 percent as of 2007.[24] Repeated lamentations have appeared in newspapers, magazines, and books, from Donald Barlett and James Steele's 1991 series "America: What Went Wrong?" in the *Philadelphia*

Inquirer to the "Downsizing of America" series in the *New York Times* in 1996; from *Trading Places* by Clyde Prestowitz in 1988, which blamed Japan for perceived American decline, to the same author's *Three Billion New Capitalists* of 2005, which blamed China and all of Asia. Recently, Lou Dobbs's book *Exporting America* in 2004 and Louis Uchitelle's *The Disposable American* in 2006 have continued in the same vein, portraying America's economy as crumbling from foreign competition and domestic fecklessness.

But the truth is very different. There were fewer jobs and less opportunity before technology and a widening global economy changed the way Americans work and live. Through all the changes of recent decades, U.S. employment has risen to its highest levels ever, unemployment has fallen to some of its lowest levels, and Americans have experienced rising living standards. The economic downturn of 2008 led to increased unemployment, true, but did not appear to promise a reversal of positive historic trends.[25]

From today's vantage point, we can see that profound changes occurred in the world economy in the final decades of the twentieth century. The historic evolution was twofold: one aspect in the explosion of technology and the other in financial innovation. This chapter has reviewed how the needs of military strategy and space exploration for communications and security spawned scientific discoveries and how technological wonders have changed the way people live and work all over the world. And the technological evolution is continuing, through uses of the Internet that not even the wildest science fiction ever dreamed of and new generation communications that have brought the world from an economy born in the nineteenth-century Industrial Revolution to a twenty-first-century economy based on information.

But this chapter has touched only lightly on the financial revolution that accompanied the technological changes and indeed made them possible. The world has seen technological changes before in history— wheels, gun powder, medicines—but almost never has it seen changes in the spread and availability of finance that have come about in the past quarter century. The futurist Alvin Toffler, author of *Future Shock* and *The Third Wave*, captures some of the magnitude of this financial change very well in his 2006 book, with Heidi Toffler, *Revolutionary Wealth: How*

It Will Be Created and How It Will Change Our Lives. The Tofflers, who live in Los Angeles, wrote: "The financial infrastructure of the United States—the beating heart, as it were, of world capitalism—is being revolutionized. Investments can be made within milliseconds and reach around the globe." What is more, there is increased access to this new diversity of financial products. Individuals, through mutual funds and tax advantaged accounts, such as 401(k) plans, can invest in an enormous variety of financial products. As a result, the Tofflers conclude, "the United States has seen [what a Federal Reserve official] refers to as the Democratization of America's capital markets." In plain English, they added, "small businesses have more sources of capital today."[26]

In this simple statement—small businesses have more sources of capital—lies a shift in the U.S. economy and, by extension, the world. In the United States, says Kenneth Kalb, founder of several high-tech companies in San Diego and currently chief executive of Analog Analytics Corp. in San Diego, there was always "admiration for risk-taking. Pioneers like Steve Jobs and Bill Gates" have always been esteemed. "But this is different," Kalb says. "The political institutions support independent business. That's why we have entrepreneurs and people can come here from other countries and raise money. No other country does that."[27]

The next chapter will explain how Southern Californians with insight and daring about the world of money changed the workings of the U.S. economy and the very people who make it grow and prosper.

The Entrepreneurial Economy,
New Capital, New Immigrants

These owners and managers are the future business leaders
of Southern California. They come from family companies
and reflect our community possibly better than the old
leadership did.

Linda Griego,
president of Rebuild L.A., 1994–97

SOUTHERN CALIFORNIA became a model for the nation
and the world in the early 1990s because it changed
from an economy led by large corporations and federal government budgets to one driven by thousands of small to medium-sized companies
and new approaches to financing. A shift of perspective occurred as entrepreneurial companies came to be seen as creators of wealth, jobs, and
industrial success. Venture capital and private equity financing became
popular. Immigrants flooded into the region during the 1990s, many
of them quick to set up family companies. Few recognized that these
happenings were part of a new economic order because, in those years,
Southern California was wracked by a series of disasters. This chapter
traces the development of this new economic landscape, through two
decades of investment drama, with stories of individuals and businesses
and portents for the future.

As the 1990s began, all of Southern California was devastated by an
economic depression caused by reduced Defense Department spending
after the end of the Cold War. Riots broke out in Los Angeles in 1992,

and brush fires burned hundreds of thousand of acres in all six counties in Southern California in 1993. Then, a major earthquake hit Los Angeles, and the government of Orange County, one of America's wealthiest neighborhoods, declared bankruptcy in 1994.[1] Initially, old thinking governed officials' reactions to the disasters. Los Angeles launched Rebuild L.A. (RLA), a nonprofit corporation that was supposed to channel investments into the poor and riot-torn areas of South Los Angeles. Public officials, including the mayor of Los Angeles and the governor of California, initially believed that supermarket companies would rebuild their stores and revive commercial vigor in the neighborhoods. But that did not happen.

Linda Griego became director of the RLA program in 1994, even as enthusiasm for the program was waning. Griego, a former Los Angeles deputy mayor—and an entrepreneur who started a television production company and owned part of a downtown restaurant and a mountain lodge—discovered a different urban economy.[2] This economy was composed of hundreds of small family companies making everything from computers to sausages and employing twenty to one hundred people. Most were struggling to cope with everyday problems of financing, marketing, and complying with rafts of regulations from city, state, and national governments. These companies' numbers and their needs had never shown up on government industrial studies. So Griego, with the aid of graduate students at UCLA, set out to count the companies and organize them into groups so she could exert more leverage with government officials and financiers.

Griego understood that these small merchants represented new growth in Southern California. She could help them get industrial development grants from the city, and that could enable them eventually to attract private financing. "These owners and managers are the future business leaders of Southern California," she told me in 1996, when the worst of the economic crisis had passed and the outlines of the future economy were visible. "They come from family companies and reflect our community possibly better than the old leadership did." During the same mid-nineties years, Orange County, San Diego, and other areas experienced a similar surge in financing and business formation.

Roots of Change in the 1970s

That new quickening in the economy did not happen overnight. Its roots lay in developments dating to the 1970s and to ideas sown and nurtured by Michael Milken, a Southern California–born financier. Milken was a prime mover in the U.S. economic restructuring that occurred during the 1970s and 1980s and during Southern California's rise to financial prominence. Born in 1946 and raised in a middle-class family in the San Fernando Valley, Milken grew up during the postwar period when Southern California blossomed. But he recalled getting a rude awakening in August 1965, when the Watts riots flared in South Central Los Angeles.[3] He ventured down to the area, still acrid with smoke and tear gas, and met a man who had lost his job because rioters had burned the factory where he worked. Yet the man had cheered on the rioters. The man was living and working in South Central Los Angeles, where African Americans had moved from the South to find community and prosperity. But as Los Angeles had grown and prospered, it seemed to many black people that prosperity was not intended for them, that they were once again the holders of a "dream deferred," to borrow a term from Langston Hughes's poem "Harlem [2]."[4]

The man told Milken that he had worked in the now-gutted factory for little pay and less regard and it wasn't his place to worry about it. That disturbed the nineteen-year-old Milken, who was majoring in mathematics at the University of California, Berkeley. "No one should be denied the right to participate in economic society, to aspire to ownership of a business rather than just a job," Milken later wrote. "Two weeks later, when I returned to Berkeley for the fall term, I changed my major from math to business and began pursuing what has been a lifelong quest: the global democratization of capital."[5] Milken studied economics and began to see discrepancies between the received wisdom of the textbooks and reality. Kings, princes, and national governments were said to be the least risky borrowers. But Milken found that august institutions and governments were far more prone to default than companies or even individuals. After graduating summa cum laude from Berkeley, he went on to the Wharton School of the University of Pennsylvania for a master's of business administration and continued his inquiries into the vagaries of who has access to credit and why. In 1969, he joined a fading but prestigious Philadelphia investment firm named Drexel Harriman Ripley and worked in the section that underwrote bonds for companies that were young and untried, or relatively weak financially.

Milken's key insight was that the risk in lending to or investing in unimposing companies was less than was indicated by the high interest rates such firms had to pay—and coincidentally the risk in supposedly golden credits was more than believed, particularly as technology and global developments were changing old certainties. In the early 1970s, for example, advances in electronics made minicomputers and then personal computers possible. Capabilities for accessing and using information moved into the hands of individuals and began to erode the dominance of IBM and other giant companies. IBM brought out its own personal computer, but IBM's suppliers, Microsoft, which made the software operating system, and Intel, which made the electronic circuitry, were propelled to economic power and prominence by that computer. The decade was a shaky time. Inflation, sparked by oil price increases, wracked the economy and affected the stock market. Corporate and public employee pension funds, which had grown during the decades after World War II, had difficulty earning the returns they needed to meet long-term obligations. As a result, the pension funds began to demand higher yields from common stock investments, forcing corporations to change, sell assets, or sell out in order to raise financial returns. In response, a whole range of investments became acceptable, from high-yield, or "junk," bonds to venture capital.

In an atmosphere of widespread change, Milken persuaded his company, which became Drexel Burnham Lambert after a 1973 merger with Burnham & Co., to help finance an upstart named Microwave Communications Inc. MCI, as it was called, had been formed by William McGowan, an entrepreneur who set up a long-distance rival to the heretofore unassailable AT&T. McGowan succeeded despite great legal and financial obstacles; Drexel financing was a big help. Milken also got Drexel to back the cable television rebel Ted Turner, whose Turner Broadcasting company grew dramatically during the 1970s, even as broadcast television networks saw their share of the national audience begin to decline.

Milken brought the Drexel firm to Southern California in 1978, opening offices for his securities trading and underwriting division in

Beverly Hills. There he put together a network that would finance numerous mergers and buyouts of public corporations using high-yield debt and complex agreements to purchase stock. In the 1980s, he helped to finance Craig McCaw, who built McCaw Cellular, a company that pioneered mobile telephone networks utilizing the technologies discovered and developed by Andrew Viterbi and Irwin Jacobs (see Chapter 2). The old monopoly AT&T was broken up in 1984, and mobile telephones continued to evolve, emerging as the world's new basic means of communication. That same year aggressive stock investors called "raiders" forced Gulf Oil to be merged into Standard Oil of California (now Chevron). In 1986, General Electric bought RCA Corp., a company that had helped to invent the radio and television industries, and the giant San Francisco–based Bank of America almost failed, following losses on loans to Mexico and other Latin American governments. Milken's warnings of risks in loans to sovereign states were borne out.

Yet amid this seeming disorder entrepreneurs built new companies in electronics and computer software. The Santa Clara Valley of northern California was reborn unofficially as Silicon Valley. Change came not only to the United States in the 1980s. Modern economies developed everywhere in Asia, including China, which had begun to reform its economy in 1978. Capital was available for new pursuits. And what appeared to be crisis was actually a constant rebirth. William Link, a leading entrepreneur and venture capital investor who founded and sold two companies and financed twenty others through Versant Ventures in Orange County, described the process succinctly decades later. "When companies get bought out, some of the people in them who owned shares found they had money," said Link in 2008. "And if they were entrepreneurial, they got the confidence to start their own companies. So industries multiplied over and over again."[6]

Attitudes changed, Milken explained to me in 2004 after Ronald Reagan's death. Milken called Reagan's election in 1980 a turning point in which American voters chose to pursue more risk-taking. "Reagan's belief in the freedom of the individual opened up access to capital for individuals and entrepreneurs in the baby boom generation," he said.

It should be noted that Milken did not become a hero for pioneering access to capital. Rather, he was a prophet without honor, as economic upheavals stemming from Japan's deflation, the breakup of the Soviet bloc, and many other dramatic changes caused a slowdown in the U.S. economy. Takeovers, buyouts, and junk bonds were blamed by corporate executives, anxious politicians, and confused media critics. Political reaction against financial innovations and corporate restructuring was swift and counterproductive. The Drexel firm went out of business; Congress forced savings and loan associations and banks to dispose of high-yield bonds, often at great loss. The bonds soon recovered and shrewd investors made killings. But Milken suffered. Prosecutors made him a scapegoat and ultimately convicted him in 1990 of violating technicalities in securities laws and he went to prison. But when he came out in 1992, Milken started on a new career participating in economic development around the world and in poor neighborhoods in the United States through the Milken Institute. He also resumed his decades-old philanthropic support of research on cancer and other life-threatening diseases, and he worked to improve education in U.S. schools (see Figure 3.1).

Figure 3.1. Michael Milken, financier and philanthropist, teaches math to an inner-city student. Photo courtesy of the Milken Institute.

In the past decade and a half, Milken's views on global economic development and finance have become widely respected, even though they are as acute and contrary as ever. "These are good times, not bad times," he says, because economic development is proceeding in so many parts of the world. At the same time, he is scornful of the financial excesses that produced the subprime mortgage crisis and credit crunch. "They simply used leverage," he said privately of investment bankers and others who devised complex mortgage derivative securities that proved unsound. "They did not create anything new or contribute anything to meet real needs."[7]

Capital for Minorities

Milken has always stoutly defended high-yield debt and other financial innovations that he introduced in the 1970s because they brought capital to people who did not have access to it before. Looking back to the early 1990s, this was certainly true in Southern California as it suffered the devastation from the defense-aerospace industry downturn. The availability of financing for small businesses allowed the region's economy to become an entrepreneurial beehive in the 1990s. The very minorities that first spurred Milken to study business now had access to capital. In 1992, even as rioters burned stretches of South Central Los Angeles, Brian Argrett, who has degrees in law and business from the University of California, Berkeley, started a small business investment firm named Fulcrum Capital Management. Its mission was to make loans to African Americans and other minorities. Changes in finance had "put more capital on the table for minority entrepreneurs and a greater openness to lending to minority-owned businesses," Argrett told me in 2002.[8] During the decade after the riots, Argrett and his associates put about $27 million to work lending to minority-led businesses, such as a firm named Chemrich that makes supermarket-brand equivalents of popular remedies like Pepto-Bismol and Robitussin. The firm succeeded in growing to $15 million in sales, Argrett said in 2007, when he was raising more than $125 million in new capital from the California Teachers' Pension System and corporate pension fund investors. "We hope to make more loans of $5 million to $75 million, amounts that can really help small to medium-sized companies grow," Argrett says.

In another example, when Linda Griego organized a food-processing industry roundtable in 1994, she introduced a score of ethnic specialty companies to each other and to city development agencies, major banks, and providers of business services. These were typically immigrant family businesses, small in size but facing the same challenges as larger outfits.

In poorer communities the focus shifted from public assistance to private initiative and public-private partnerships. After the Los Angeles riots, Bernard Kinsey, a retired top executive from Xerox, was on the board of RLA. He saw to it that entrepreneurial thinking got a hearing. He helped John Hope Bryant organize a Bankers Bus Tour to take bankers around the blighted areas of South Central Los Angeles. Bryant knew that all bankers under a federal law called the Community Reinvestment Act (CRA) had to make a percentage of their loans to poor areas, for housing or small businesses. So he took bankers to the devastated areas to show them a ready-made outlet for their CRA obligation loans. "The people need a hand up, not a handout," Bryant said repeatedly to me in interviews and to busloads of bankers in those midyears of the 1990s. It was the rallying cry of his Project HOPE, which brought capital into the community.[9]

Bryant was also involved with Los Angeles' first African Methodist Episcopal (AME) Church, where the Rev. Cecil "Chip" Murray founded FAME Renaissance to help inner-city dwellers attract mortgage loans. Bryant, who went on to become bishop of all AME churches in the western United States, instructed borrowers on how to maintain a mortgage and thus generate a credit rating. "Education is the ultimate poverty eradication tool," he would say as we drove around poor, but house-proud, inner-city neighborhoods.

In those years, small business lost its amateur image and instead became a focus for sophisticated investors. For example, Riordan, Lewis & Haden (RLH), an investment firm formed by lawyer and venture investor Richard Riordan (later mayor of Los Angeles), backed Orange County entrepreneur Mary Ellen Weaver in 1994. Weaver had built a staffing business called Data Processing Resources Corp. (DPRC) that found skilled employees for high-technology companies. A one-time temporary typist in a small Newport Beach firm, Weaver saw firsthand the phenomenal growth of the computer information industry. She founded DPRC in 1985. "There is a shortage of 350,000 information specialists in the United States," she told me in 1998, when her business had grown to great size. When RLH invested in Weaver's company, it had $35 million in annual revenues, and the story perfectly illustrated the new environment in Southern California at that time: a female entrepreneur, with a relatively small company in business services, could attract financial backing from investors of private equity capital. With help from those investors in making acquisitions and securing executive talent, Weaver's firm grew to more than $300 million in revenues by 1999 when she and RLH sold it to a large software company for almost $500 million.[10]

Information Technology as Engine

San Diego's recession in the early 1990s was devastating, but the city's reaction was different from that of Los Angeles. In pondering what her city should do, then-mayor Susan Golding was a step ahead of her time. She noticed that the San Diego area had an extraordinary amount of fiber optic and television cable lines so that TV and telecommunications transmissions could cope with mountainous terrain. Also, decades of investment from military and space programs had laid a foundation for a new industry. "A lot of technology was not accessible, the Internet was not being used," she told me in 1996. "We knew that San Diego's economic future depended on upgrading our telecommunications capabilities." So she launched a program to link city government, businesses, schools, hospitals, and libraries through computer-telecommunications networks. Her venturesome plan worked. By the mid-1990s, the San Diego area had become home to 200 telecommunications firms, 350 software companies, and 200 biotechnology and medical outfits. Almost all of them were small companies, financed by venture investors and aided by research support at local universities and scientific institutes.[11]

Thus, gradually, a region that began the 1990s fearing for its future, adapted to new economic patterns, as investment flowed to enterprise. Today, Southern California is astoundingly dynamic, a vibrant and reassuring example of an entrepreneurial economy. The region is filled with small companies—those with fewer than ninety-nine employees. There are 536,758 such companies in the six-county region, according to the Los Angeles County Economic Development Corp., which also found in a 2007 survey that there are more than 780,000 self-employed, single-person firms[12] (see Figure 3.2). That is more than any other state on both counts—and the majority share of entrepreneurial businesses for all of California.

Investment comes to Southern California at a furious pace these days. More than $3 billion in venture capital was invested in the region's fledgling companies in 2008, placing it second in the United States behind Silicon Valley for that form of investment. Private equity investors are funneling vast amounts of money to Southern California to take advantage of the region's expertise in small to medium-sized companies. In 2008, even as worries mounted about a global credit crunch and a crisis in mortgage securities, investment conferences in Southern California attracted thousands of venture investors eager to hear from hundreds of small to medium-sized companies. Roth Capital Partners in Orange County featured fifty companies from China. "Today's China companies are just like the small entrepreneurial outfits with a lot of promise that we helped bring along in the early 1990s," said Byron Roth, founder of the twenty-five-year-old investment bank. The story was similar at the technology conference of Montgomery & Co., another small investment

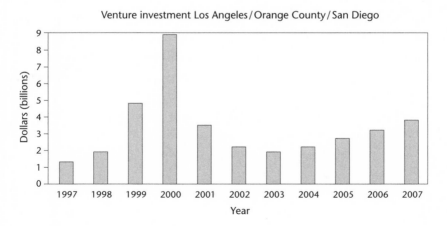

Figure 3.2. Venture capital that has come to Los Angeles, Orange County, and San Diego over the course of a decade. Sources: Author's calculations based on PricewaterhouseCoopers "MoneyTree Report."

bank that attracted 750 investors and 160 small telecommunications companies to its meeting in March 2008. "It is a good time for mobile phone companies," said James W. Montgomery, chairman of Montgomery, which has been raising money for small companies in media, communications, and health care for twenty years, "because the infrastructure of the Internet has been built out. So companies selling entertainment and services for phones can innovate on the Internet."[13]

"There is a lot of money in Southern California," Michael Tennenbaum has told me repeatedly. Tennenbaum, who founded Tennenbaum Capital Partners in 1996, is one of the pioneers of Southern California finance. As a partner at Bear Stearns, he backed entrepreneurial outfits like the Jenny Craig weight-loss company in 1983. In little more than a decade, his firm has raised $5 billion from national and international institutions. His twenty-seven investment professionals put the money to work in such transactions as a $69 million loan to Integra Telecom, a provider of Internet and telecommunications services to small companies in five western states.[14]

When Tennenbaum, who came to California from Georgia, talks of "a lot of money" in Southern California, he is referring to fortunes earned in the growth of the Los Angeles region after World War II and to other fortunes made by people who have come to this region from all corners of the earth. The totals of wealth created in contemporary Southern California would be in the hundreds of billions of dollars, if anybody could calculate the amounts. The *Wall Street Journal* gave a sense of the region's wealth in a 2007 calculation that found 477,204 millionaires in Los Angeles, Orange, and San Diego counties—more than 5 percent of a national total of 9.3 million people with a net worth of more than $1 million, not including the value of houses. Los Angeles County led all U.S. counties with 261,081 millionaires.[15]

What is it about Southern California that attracts enterprising people? Tennenbaum ticks off well-known features like the climate and smart public investments in universities, before citing a most interesting reason: "This area didn't have so many old families. Many people here are the first generation to come to California; they are immigrants or Americans who came here to seek a fortune. They are not held back by concentrations of family money, or social status, or any of that."

He is referring to people like Eli Broad, born in Detroit, who built Kaufman & Broad and then took over and built the retirement finance company SunAmerica in Los Angeles. Broad and his wife Edythe, through the Broad Foundations, have given billions of dollars to biotechnology institutes at universities here and elsewhere and contributed mightily to cultural institutions. Lately he has been the driving force in building part of a whole new downtown for Los Angeles. Another billionaire, Philip Anschutz, came from Denver, built the Staples Center athletic arena, a regional oil pipeline, and a center for world-class soccer in the region. One of Anschutz's companies, the AEG Group, is also building hotels, theaters, broadcast facilities, and a museum in Los Angeles. In Orange County, Donald Bren, a Los Angeles native and head of the Irvine Company, has built industrial and commercial complexes and spearheaded the growth of the University of California, Irvine. In San Diego County, Irwin Jacobs, the Massachusetts-born founder of Qualcomm, has become a major force of philanthropy and encouragement in civic and economic life (see Chapter 2).

Immigrant Energy

Of course, the most extraordinary fact about Southern California in recent decades has been the tremendous growth of immigration, from everywhere. The region has received large flows of immigration from Mexico and significant numbers of skilled immigrants from Canada, which is a large trading partner of California. (See Chapter 4 for a more thorough discussion of the Latino population of Southern California and its growing importance for the United States.)

Asia is the other major source of immigrants, with hundreds of thousands of people bringing billions of dollars to Southern California. These newcomers are investing capital and more, their lives and families, in the U.S. economy. And often these immigrant groups form ventures that span the Pacific, with investment and business activity in the new country and the old. The largest of the groups from Asia are Chinese immigrants, their offspring, and Chinese Americans, who number about 1 million in Southern California—out of more than 2 million nationwide. Chapter 5 explores the large and varied economic role that Chinese immigrants are playing in this region. Meanwhile, this chapter discusses many other groups from Asia, takes a look at Canadian involvement in the region, and presents a review of the Japanese in America, the people who perhaps more than any other have demonstrated the perils of injustice and yet also the breadth and hopeful reality of the new world economy.

The Korean Way

The Korean community of Southern California, which by conservative estimates numbers about four hundred thousand, swelled in the two decades after the Immigration Act of 1965. Many of those immigrants were well educated; some had worked in other countries as miners and nurses before coming to the United States. "Koreans were highly educated in their country of origin, often well endowed with money upon arrival in the United States, and commonly middle or upper middle class in social origin," Ivan Light and Edna Bonacich reported in their 1988 book *Immigrant Entrepreneurs.*[16] Korean immigrants also were more entrepreneurial than any other immigrant group. One reason is the tradition in Korean communities of rotating credit funds, or *kyes*, in which people pool money, lend to one person, who puts it to use and then pays it back, making the loan available for the next *kye* member, and so on. In this way, capital is available to fund numerous small businesses.

Then the Korean business community in Southern California stepped up to a higher level. During the Asian financial crisis of 1997–98, giant corporations or *chaebol* in Korea reorganized operations and reduced staff. Executives in their early fifties had to take early retirement, but usually with a tidy severance package to add to their already substantial savings. Businesspeople of that economic and social rank had often sent their children to America for an education. Now, many of these men and their wives decided to move themselves, and they brought serious capital with them—$150,000 to $500,000 each and even more. The amounts are significant because an immigrant coming to the United States with $150,000, who promises to employ an American, gains the right to stay in the country. An immigrant who brings in $500,000 and promises to hire ten Americans qualifies for a permanent residence "green card." The effect in Southern California has been increasingly evident in the past decade. The Korean community in Los

Angeles and neighboring Orange County became known for wielding a lot of capital. Four major Korean banks, housed in Korean-owned office buildings on Wilshire Boulevard, grew to an imposing $8 billion in total assets. Korean immigrants bought coffee shop concessions in the lobbies of those office buildings, paying more than $100,000 for such concessions and hiring local youngsters to wipe counters and do other chores—thereby raising their U.S. residency status because they were employers.[17]

Korean businesspeople became very active in commercial real estate, with one Korean-owned company, David Lee's Jamison Properties, becoming the largest commercial property owner in Los Angeles County. Lee's career offers one of the clearest illustrations of the growth of Korean investment in the Los Angeles region. He came to the United States from Seoul in 1971 at age seventeen and trained in internal medicine at Northwestern University Medical School. Lee bought his first office building on Wilshire Boulevard in 1995 when Los Angeles was still under a cloud in the aftermath of the 1992 riots, during which Korean storeowners in particular were attacked. After the brush fires in 1993 and earthquake in 1994, insurance companies were selling half-empty buildings at knockdown prices, feeling that it was impossible that the economy would revive.

But Lee knew that a hidden market existed among Korean immigrant entrepreneurs. Lacking a credit rating in America, but rich with severance pay, they had cash to pay rent for office space. On behalf of himself and eight other Korean immigrant doctors and dentists, who organized under the name Jamison Properties to make tax-deferred investments, Lee paid $6 million for his first office building on Wilshire Boulevard. A decade later, the building was worth five times that purchase price as Lee and his investing associates bought a score more office buildings on Wilshire and a great range of real estate throughout the metropolitan area.

In 2006, Jamison Properties owned seventy office buildings, thirteen medical buildings, and six shopping centers, together worth more than $3 billion. The company is now backed by one hundred investors, "90 percent of them still Korean," Lee told me. He promises those investors a 15 percent annual return and has achieved it partly by cutting maintenance costs on the buildings but mostly by sitting back and watching property prices rise along with the Southern California economy. Patience is his long suit. "We invest on a six-to-seven-year cycle," Lee says, "where most investors are on a three-to-five-year cycle."

Lee has a daughter and two sons at the University of Southern California and another son in high school. If he were back in South Korea and able to amass so much property and wealth, Lee might now be grooming his children to carry on a family business. But America is different from the old country, Lee acknowledged, when I asked him whether his children would join him in the business. "If they like money, they will," he responded with a smile. "If they don't like money, they will be nonprofit." The answer reflects the pride the Korean community takes in the academic achievements of its hard-working children, who are already ascending professional ranks.

Koreans, even in a relatively short time in the United States, have become known for drive and dedication. Charles Rim, a Korean-born, UCLA-educated accountant, offered a theory rooted in history when I spoke to him in 2005. "Koreans are like many people who were poor and colonized for centuries; they want to prove something to themselves and to others," he said. Rim, founder and owner of an accounting firm, is a good example of that drive. In 2007 he invested in a new supermarket in Torrance that caters to Korean tastes, and he has also invested in land for residential development in Ventura and Santa Barbara counties.

Behind all the activity has been fresh money coming from South Korea. "The Korean economy has a trade and financial surplus," explains Sung Won Sohn, economist and now-retired president and chief executive of Hanmi Bank in Los Angeles, which has grown to $3.8 billion in assets from $300 million in the past sixteen years. "The Korean government is making it possible, and encouraging, people to invest outside Korea," rather than have excess funds spark inflation at home. Sohn estimates that more than $30 billion in such investment funds have flowed into this region from Korea in recent years. "They come here to invest in this wonderful real estate," he says of the vast expanse of Southern California. Sohn, son of a banker in Korea, earned a doctorate in economics from the University of Pittsburgh, served as a senior economist on President Richard Nixon's

Council of Economic Advisers, and spent thirty-one years as the chief economist at Wells Fargo Bank. He came to Hanmi, the largest of Los Angeles' Korean banks, in 2005 because he says the community of Korean and other ethnic businesses is now large enough to need the complex services a big bank can offer, such as letters of credit on global transactions, cash management, and so forth. Also, he came because investment ties between Seoul and the Los Angeles region are expanding.

Sohn's career and those of two other Korean Americans illustrate how swiftly it is possible for newcomers to experience economic and political success in Southern California's global economy—and how the region benefits from the newcomers' energy and enthusiasm. Stewart Kim, for example, is a Korean American who owns a Los Angeles investment bank that specializes in transactions between America and Asia. He was born in Ohio in 1981, where his parents had moved from Korea to study at Ohio University and Oberlin College. After taking degrees from Dartmouth and the Wharton School at Penn, Kim became a managing director of Merrill Lynch in New York, but in 2003 he decided to move to Southern California because the Korean community was building up. He explained that he started PGP Capital Advisors because "Korean businesses need access to institutional capital markets and major corporate relationships." Kim took on Latino and Chinese entrepreneurs as advisers and a business partner from the "mainstream" or nonethnic investment banking world to give his firm broad access to financial communities. In 2007, Kim's company engineered a deal in which golfer Jack Nicklaus's Golden Bear International formed a partnership with a New York bank and received an investment of $145 million to distribute Nicklaus brand golf equipment and golf course design services all over Asia. "Jack could have picked any Wall Street firm, but he chose us," Kim said to me, with understandable pride in the accomplishment. Kim also serves on the affordable housing commission of Los Angeles mayor Antonio Villaraigosa.

Sabrina Kay's story illustrates even more how the Korean community is entering the broad U.S. economic and political community. Kay (shown in Figure 3.3) emigrated from Korea with her parents in 1982 when she was seventeen. Attracted to Los Angeles' fashion industry, she considered designing while studying at California State University,

Figure 3.3. Entrepreneur Sabrina Kay appearing in Seoul at a fashion show that she organized. Courtesy of the Sabrina Kay Organization.

Long Beach, but ultimately had a better idea. Seeing that there were opportunities among the 11,500 local apparel firms that specialize in the design, cutting, or sewing of garments, Kay decided that a school to teach the new techniques of computer-aided design and manufacturing would be a good idea. She had a source of capital in that she could borrow $500,000 from her parents, who had opened a successful retail store upon their arrival in the United States. So in 1991, she opened California Design College, charging students who wanted to upgrade their skills $12,000 a year—which was obtainable through federal loans and grants for job training. "I wanted to establish a technical school that would teach job skills without all the other academic courses," Kay recalled in 2003. She worked hard and made the school a success, bringing in $6 million a year from five hundred students after a decade in operation. Then, with career education seen as a growth business, a large Pittsburgh company named Education Management Corp. bought Kay's business in 2003 for $15 million.

Kay didn't relax on her millions. She enrolled in the master's of business administration program at the University of Southern California and got involved in Korean American organizations and in the Young Presidents' Organization—a major networking group in entrepreneurial business nationally. She cofounded Premier Business Bank with David Lee in 2006. She also got involved in city government, taking an appointment to the Los Angeles Planning Commission in 2005, and worked on trade missions. She organized fashion shows in Shanghai and Seoul for Mayor Villaraigosa's trade mission to Asia in 2006. Kay is now involved in bringing California fashions to China and has gone back to career education by purchasing Fremont College, which specializes in training for paralegal work and occupations in banking, real estate, and health care. Amid a breakneck schedule, Kay is pursuing a doctorate at the Wharton School and has earned a master's degree in higher education. And she still manages to lecture at local universities on rising Asian women.

The Vietnamese Struggle

Of all the new Asian immigrant groups in Southern California, the Vietnamese came here with the least in money and possessions, as they fled the rule of a Communist government in the wake of the Vietnam War. Over time, they built a beehive of commerce in two cities in Orange County—Westminster and Garden Grove—that are now home to more than 150,000 Vietnamese Americans and more than five thousand entrepreneurial businesses, including two relatively new Vietnamese-owned banks.[18] Until 2005, banking needs of Vietnamese immigrant companies were served by Bank of America and Wells Fargo or by Chinese and Korean "ethnic" banks. But now, Vietnamese-backed banks are open because "Little Saigon" in the Orange County communities of Garden Grove and Westminster is seeing more business connections with the old homeland and a vibrant, if nominally Communist, entrepreneurial sector back in Vietnam. Saigon National Bank, for example, was founded in 2005 by Kiem Nguyen, owner of one of the largest supermarkets in Little Saigon, as well as fertilizer and plastics businesses in Vietnam. Another institution, first Vietnamese American Bank, raised more than

$11 million in capital and opened its doors in May 2005. "When Vietnamese businesspeople come to this bank, they can deal with the bank president personally, they can come home," Hieu Nguyen, the bank's president, told me in 2005.

More than sentiment is involved. The new banks answer a need in America's Vietnamese population, which numbers half a million people in California. Reliable estimates say that some $8 billion a year in cash remittances, trade in goods, and services flow between ethnic Vietnamese in the United States and relatives and business partners in Vietnam. Sending cash to relatives through informal transfer agencies can be expensive for the families—and a source of concern for bank regulators worried about irregularities. That's one reason state and federal authorities welcomed the new banks. Also, there is simply a lot of business to do. The economy in Vietnam, a country of 84 million people, has been growing at more than 7 percent a year for almost a decade. A bilateral trade agreement with the United States in 2001 has spurred that growth, says George Baker, a vice president of Far East National Bank, a Los Angeles institution that is owned by a Taiwanese banking company. Baker opened a Far East National branch in Ho Chi Minh City (formerly Saigon) in 2004. "Few people realize," he told me in 2005, "that Vietnam is one of the world's largest exporters of coffee and rice and that it has special capabilities in garments and high-tech components."

For example, Jocelyn Tran, a veteran of twenty years in Southern California's fashion industry, runs a subsidiary of Limited Brands in her native Vietnam and ships more than 200 million garments a year to the company's chains, which include Victoria's Secret, The Limited, and Henri Bendel stores. "China does large, mass merchandise orders but for hand-beading and intricate needlework, Vietnamese workers' skills give us a good niche," says Tran, who makes her U.S. home in Orange County. The Vietnamese in Orange County exemplify the billowing opportunities of the international economy—and also the adaptability and industriousness of the new Vietnamese Americans. One more story underlines that industriousness.

Most Vietnamese in Orange County cheer progress in the old country, even though the bitterness of immigrants who fled the aftermath of a lost civil war has not entirely faded. One still sees Vietnam Republic flags—three red stripes on a yellow field—waving in some front yards. But business beckons. "I think it is great that we have first Vietnamese Bank for our community," says Paul Nguyen, owner of Pacific Machinery Co., in Garden Grove. However, he isn't doing business in Vietnam for his own company. His reasons and the success of Pacific Machinery speak loudly of the spirit that enabled Vietnamese immigrants to build prosperous communities in the United States—and undoubtedly are helping other Vietnamese build entrepreneurial companies in the Socialist Republic of Vietnam.

A first lieutenant in South Vietnam's army and educated with U.S. government help in the United States, Nguyen was imprisoned in Vietnam for ten years when Hanoi took over. "When I came out I was 90 pounds," says the now-140-pound Nguyen, who came to America in 1985 at age thirty-seven. Nguyen worked in machine shops and taught himself computer-aided design and manufacturing. In 1992, he opened his own company and qualified as a minority contractor to supply aircraft parts to Boeing. "I work hard, twelve to thirteen hours a day," Nguyen told me in 2005. "Today, I own three buildings." He also owns a company employing seventy people with annual revenues of $10 million, supplying Boeing, Northrop Grumman, and Raytheon. And he was ready for the next phase. "I am going to invest $5 million to buy a larger plant and machinery so I can supply Boeing's new planes," Nguyen said. He did invest the money that year; raising the capital was no obstacle, he reported. "Bankers are happy to lend to me," Nguyen said. "The people from Boeing say, 'Paul, you are the American dream.' I say thank you America."

Indus Enterprise

Much debate goes on these days about the role of India in the outsourcing of U.S. jobs, a place where computer-savvy people work at a fraction of U.S. wages. But the creation of wealth in the United States by immigrant businesspeople from India and Pakistan is almost never mentioned in such debates. It should be. The Indus Entrepreneurs offers one of the most remarkable examples of immigration, international business, and the Internet combining to enlarge the economies of California, the

United States, and the world. TiE, as the organization calls itself, was founded in 1992 in California by Pakistani and Indian entrepreneurs. The name comes from the eighteen-hundred-mile Indus River that flows from the Himalayas through Pakistan and into India, thus symbolizing for the entrepreneurial immigrants to Southern California a peaceful vision for the two countries that have quarreled and fought each other for the past sixty years.[19]

Safi Qureshey, a Pakistani immigrant and cofounder of AST Research in Irvine, was one of the prime movers in the Indus Entrepreneurs. The other was Suhas Patil, an immigrant from India who founded Cirrus Logic in Silicon Valley. They saw the organization as a mutual aid network to help other Indian and Pakistani immigrant entrepreneurs with contacts and advice. Their effort bore fruit. TiE now has ten thousand members in ten countries. It is estimated that TiE members have created more than $250 billion in new wealth in the United States through their encouragement of startup businesses, said Shivbir Grewal, a prominent Orange County lawyer who is from India originally. To put that in context, it means that enterprising TiE members in a few decades in America have created the equivalent of the gross national product of Denmark or Indonesia.

Now TiE activities have evolved beyond help for immigrant hopefuls to development of companies in business services and technology with simultaneous operations in South Asia and the United States, on what some call the Indo-U.S. Corridor. Qureshey, for example, founded Avaz Networks, a semiconductor and software firm, in Irvine and Islamabad, to foster Internet development in Pakistan. "In every city in Pakistan you see Internet companies developing," he told me in 2002. "And many of the companies are extensions of India's successful software firms." Sabeer Bhatia, as another example, came from Bangalore in 1988 to study at Caltech and Stanford University. He cofounded Hotmail, the e-mail service provider, in 1996 and sold it to Microsoft in 1998 for $400 million. After that he invested in startup companies in California and today is organizing a new technology and research city in India that he envisions benefiting from American innovations in business organization and financing. "The great assets of American business and technology are the capital markets which back new ventures," Bhatia said in 2006.

Increasing innovation will be the rule, Apurv Bagri predicts. Bagri, a senior member of TiE who is based in London, told me in 2006 of the organization's vision. "You will see Indian investment in America and other countries, as well as the world investing in India," Bagri said, putting succinctly India's role in the global economy and the role of Southern California and the United States. The point is that living standards and industrial capabilities are rising in countries that never knew much of either before. It is human progress facilitated by the availability and unfettered investment of capital. Southern California's living standards and those of the whole United States have benefited from those flows of investment.

The Neighbors: Canada and Japan

Two other countries have had extraordinary effects on the economy of Southern California. The first is Canada, a country that often is not viewed in the same light as China or Europe or even Mexico, the other North American partner. Canada, for example, has 278 companies in Los Angeles County alone, about three times the 97 companies from China and Hong Kong. The Canadian government reckons that Canada's trade with the United States creates more than 800,000 jobs in California.[20] Canada, which has about the same population as California, avidly supports research and joint projects with universities in California. The truth is, as the Southern California economy has grown, Canada has become a partner in that growth. It hosts production for the region's movie and television industries in much the same way that Canada has always been a partner of Detroit's automakers, sharing production across the border. The Los Angeles film industry complains that TV shows filmed and taped in Canada are runaway productions, but companies such as Infinity Media Canada of Vancouver, which helps to finance and produce entertainment, show that the relationship is often symbiotic. The relationship is growing, too, as TC PipeLines is building lines from Baja California to Riverside and Imperial counties in California to deliver liquefied natural gas from Mexico to this region.

Far more poignant, and of far greater consequence economically, is the long history of Japanese relations with the economy of Southern California and the United States. The story begins with immigration during the late nineteenth century to Hawaii and California by Japanese men to work in agriculture. Uniquely for Asian immigrants at that time, Japanese women also immigrated as "picture brides" who would be betrothed in Japan on the basis of a photograph and come to the United States to meet their husbands for the first time. The result was that Japanese settlements became communities of families. And their abilities in agriculture led to reclamation and productivity of swamp and desert from northern and central California down through the Imperial Valley east of San Diego. During that early time, Kinji Ushijima, who became known as George Shima, built great holdings, as did others. As the immigrants succeeded—indeed as Japanese in America became first- and second-generation residents of the United States—they dreamed of taking their place in the society to which they were contributing ideas, innovation, and productivity. But those dreams were denied. A U.S. Supreme Court decision in 1922 ruled against a Japanese immigrant's application for citizenship because he was not "Caucasian," and the abhorrent Immigration Act of 1924 effectively forbade further Japanese immigration. Furthermore, Japanese residents who were born and had lived for generations in the United States by 1941 were interned during World War II.[21]

In the aftermath, there was no quick recovery to the fortunes of Japanese farmers who had lost their land and livelihoods. Many sons and daughters of Japanese Americans, some born in internment camps, worked diligently and became professionals in medicine and education and with time respected holders of political and judicial office. Ironically, William Ouchi, a scholar born in 1943 in Honolulu, came to write books such as *Theory Z: How American Management Can Meet the Japanese Challenge* during the 1980s when companies from Japan were beating U.S. industry competitively. Ouchi, a professor at UCLA Anderson School of Management, also published *Making Schools Work* (2003), a plan to solve America's continuing crisis in elementary and secondary education.

Fortunately, Southern California benefited greatly, and the U.S. economy ultimately was improved by the rise of Japanese industries that rebuilt themselves with U.S. help after the war. In the 1970s and 1980s, Japanese companies began to contribute investments, employment, and technological advances to the U.S. economy, a tradition that continues to this day. first, Japan sent radios and televisions made by Sony; cars made by Toyota, Nissan, and Honda; and televisions made by Mitsubishi and Matsushita (Panasonic). Then they sent investment. Sony Corp. was early to expand in the United States, ultimately investing more than $7 billion in two movie studios in Los Angeles and factories and research centers in San Diego and San Jose, among other places. In the 1970s, Toyota, Honda, and Nissan set up U.S. headquarters in Southern California, where their executives and families felt welcome and familiar. Ultimately, the Japanese companies led a phalanx of foreign car producers making vehicles mostly in the Southeast and Midwest, from Ohio to Alabama. Toyota, to take one example, has invested $15 billion in the United States to date and employs thirty-three thousand people here. It has U.S. headquarters in Torrance and manufacturing plants in California, Kentucky, and several other states. And, Toyota is looking to the future by opening an automotive research center at the University of Michigan in Ann Arbor, home ground of a century of Detroit's engineering knowledge. "They're putting a Toyota executive training facility right there near the campus," says a U.S. expert, "so that the brightest students can walk right over." (General Motors and Ford, meanwhile, though troubled in North American operations, are expanding in China, where GM is the leading foreign car maker.)[22]

The idea that Toyota and Sony have all but displaced giant American firms in leadership and innovation in their respective fields teaches a useful lesson about the changing world, and that is that modern Southern California and the United States have prospered by welcoming new technology and flows of capital—and new people. People from many lands have enriched Southern California, as we've seen. But in the past decade or so, many immigrants to Southern California and other parts of the United States have come from Mexico and Latin America, some of them crossing the border without legal papers. This has made immigration once again a heated political issue in the United States, even as Latino labor and enterprise have enriched the economy. So the next chapter tells of the present reality and great promise of Latino Americans.

4   Latin American Immigrants
       Spur the Economy

I believe very strongly that the energy of people coming here
[to Southern California] makes this in many ways, in our
lifetime, the center of gravity of the world economy.

Enrique Hernandez Jr.,
president, Inter-Con Security Systems

SINCE SOUTHERN CALIFORNIA has received a surge
of immigrants from Latin America and Asia, Enrique
"Rick" Hernandez Jr. sees in the region "opportunity greater than in
any other part of the country." Hernandez, whose grandparents emigrated from Mexico after the 1911 revolution, sees the immigrants as
"new people with new ideas who want to be successful—a confluence of
entrepreneurial companies. We're very lucky to be here."[1]

The whole United States is experiencing a surge of immigration,
one that has lasted more than a decade. By official statistics, more than
12 percent of the national population is foreign born, the highest percentage of immigrants since the great waves came from southern and
eastern Europe from 1900 to 1910. And if the 11 million people estimated to live in this country illegally are taken into account, the immigrant percentage rises to more than 15 percent of the population.[2] The
new waves come predominantly from Mexico, Central America, South
America, the Caribbean, and the populous nations of Asia—particularly
China and Korea. Beyond doubt, the center of this era's immigration is
Los Angeles and its surrounding region.

Hernandez is a quietly influential businessman in Los Angeles and across the country. He is president and chief executive of Inter-Con Security Systems, a firm based in Pasadena that protects U.S. government and private property around the world. He also is chairman of Nordstrom stores and a director of McDonald's and Wells Fargo. He is a leader in the Los Angeles community, former head of its police commission, and a trustee of Children's Hospital, the California HealthCare Foundation, and local committees for Harvard College, where he received his undergraduate education before earning a law degree from Harvard University. He is also a trustee of Loyola High School and Notre Dame University—a backer of education as the "key to advancement for everybody." His belief in the economic benefit that immigrants bring is not mere sentiment.

Hernandez understands that California and the United States have moved on to the next phase in the modern immigration drama, even as many parts of the Midwest and South seem bewildered by or angry at a rise in new immigrants from Mexico and Latin America. The real story is one of Americanization, not immigration. Some 60 percent of the 12.5 million California Latino residents are American offspring and descendants of immigrants. A comparable figure holds for all the 44 million Latinos in the country; 26.1 million or just about 60 percent were born in the United States, according to the Pew Hispanic Center, a nonpartisan think tank supported by Philadelphia's Pew Charitable Trusts[3] (Table 4.1). Also, a majority of foreign-born residents are fast becoming naturalized citizens. Most Latinos are moving into the mainstream of the U.S. economy, in white- and blue-collar jobs, in middle manager ranks in finance and industry, and as entrepreneurs with their own companies. Furthermore, economic ties are growing between Latino families here and in the countries of their forebears. Timing means a lot. Just as California—and especially the Los Angeles region—led the nation in receiving Latino immigrants in the 1990s, today Southern California shows the United States what the restless energy of young people fresh to new possibilities can mean for the economy, as well as for political and social life. This new Mesoamerica is a good and growing story that I will tell through tales of family businesses and community organizations that are building a regional and national economic presence.

Table 4.1. Latino U.S.A.: Eleven states with largest Latino population and percentage Latino in each

State	Latino population	Total population	Percentage latino
California	13,087,981	36,457,549	35.9
Texas	8,379,992	23,507,783	35.6
Florida	3,642,610	18,089,889	20.1
New York	3,139,787	19,306,183	16.3
Illinois	1,889,528	12,831,970	14.7
Arizona	1,796,643	6,166,318	29.1
New Jersey	1,360,784	8,724,560	15.6
Colorado	927,453	4,753,377	19.5
New Mexico	874,125	1,954,599	44.7
Georgia	695,521	9,363,941	7.4
Nevada	605,059	2,495,529	24.2

SOURCE: Author's calculations based on data from Pew Hispanic Center tabulations of the U.S. Census Bureau's 2006 American Community Survey.

Need and Discord

Amid controversy about illegal aliens and whether new Americans will assimilate as other ethnic groups have in the past, it is important to understand several aspects of immigration's long history in and contributions to the U.S. economy, especially in terms of labor, discord, and resolution.

Immigration has supplied the labor to build railroads and steel mills, bridges and tunnels, automobiles and airplanes. The country needs new active workers because the baby boom generation, the 78 million people born between 1946 and 1964, is already declining in the workforce and will soon retire in great numbers. During the next two decades, the ratio of older, retired citizens to active workers in California will rise by one-third, to 350 seniors for every 1,000 workers. Nationally, this ratio will rise to more than one retired person for every two-and-a-half active workers. One hundred years ago, there were ten workers for every retired person. If new immigrant families were not replenishing the human capital with high birthrates as they are, the economy would be in danger of retreat, says Dowell Myers, professor of policy and planning at the University of Southern California, in his book *Immigrants and*

Boomers. "The economy depends on workers who can hold jobs; filling those jobs is a matter of finding enough people who are old enough to have acquired suitable training and who have not retired from the labor force," Myers writes. "Without those workers, the economy cannot grow and may, in fact, shrink."[4]

Another scholar, George J. Borjas of Harvard University, contends that while the United States may need immigrants, it should no longer open its doors to just any workers. The need of the new economy is for skilled workers, he argues. "A strong case can be made that the social welfare of the United States would increase if the country adopted an immigration policy that favored the entry of skilled workers," Borjas wrote in his book *Heaven's Door.* Borjas, who immigrated to the United States from Cuba in 1962 when he was twelve years old, suggests that the United States could institute a point system like that of Canada that assesses immigrants on the basis of age, skills, and other criteria.[5]

Such ideas will almost certainly be a major topic of future debate in Congress. It is equally certain that debate over policies will arouse controversy, because immigration always has. Discord followed waves of newcomers in the past, as it is doing today. A recollection of how lumpy the "melting pot" has been lends perspective to the present, in which Southern California has become the new "golden door" for immigrants. The current immigration wave began with the Immigration and Nationality Act of 1965, or the Hart-Celler Act, which opened the way for Asian immigration and for the first time addressed and set terms on Latin American immigration. After passage of the 1965 law, California became the chief port of entry for immigrants to the United States, replacing New York. This contemporary wave is the fourth in U.S. history, and all four periods demonstrate a pattern: a tendency for periods of openness to be followed by periods of xenophobia and restriction. Our history is one of constant controversy, in which more open immigration was a long time coming.

The colonizers who started the country were the first immigrants in a long wave that ran to 1820. Controversies about religious beliefs led these newcomers to settle in various states. From the 1840s to 1860, immigrants from Europe—Germany, France, and Sweden—who had been facing political upheavals at home came to America. Also, hundreds of thousands of Irish, fleeing the potato famine of the 1840s, flooded into the United States. That influx brought potential soldiers to fight in the Civil War but also brought huge populations of mostly poor and uneducated people to American cities and helped spark the 1863 draft riots in New York City, five days of some of the worst urban riots in U.S. history, with 120 people killed and 2,000 injured, according to historian James M. McPherson.[6] The next wave, from 1880 to 1920, brought immigrants from southern and eastern Europe to help build the expanding industrial economy. These newcomers somewhat changed America's ethnic mix and so prompted a backlash that resulted in the Immigration Act of 1924, or the Johnson-Reed Act, which reinforced bans on Asian immigrants and practically closed off immigration from Italy and Greece through quotas that favored northern European stock. Immigration then fell during the Great Depression and World War II. Postwar immigration rose but was restricted again by the Immigration and Nationality Act of 1952, or the McCarran-Walter Act, which confirmed discriminatory quotas but ended total exclusion of Asian peoples. The 1952 law, however, said nothing about migration from Mexico, which was then rising and encountering hostility in the Southwest.[7]

Finally, in 1965, the Hart-Celler Act did away with quotas, opening the way for Asian and Latin American families to come to the United States. Latinos had a head start as people from Mexico and Central America had been moving to California since the first missionaries and rancheros during the nineteenth century. In 1970, the Latino American population was about 12 percent of California's total. By 1990 Latinos had grown to 26 percent, and they are projected to be 38.7 percent of the state's total population by 2010.[8]

That brings us to our third key aspect of immigration: resolution. The assimilation of Latino groups today is clouded and confused by the presence of unauthorized or illegal immigrants in the United States. According to the Pew Hispanic Center, 11.1 million unauthorized immigrants are in the country, 2.5 to 2.75 million in California. But the picture is not a simple one. Almost 30 percent of undocumented immigrants are U.S. citizens because they are children born to parents who entered illegally. And one-quarter of these people have some college education and undoubtedly are filling more than minimum wage jobs.[9]

It is a fact that more illegal immigrants entered the United States from 1995 to 1999 than at any time in the previous two decades. Many came from Mexico because that country's economy nearly collapsed in 1995 when the peso was devalued once again. At the same time, unskilled jobs were opening up across the United States. But the rapid influx aroused opposition in large areas of the country that had not received Latino immigrants previously. Alarmists about illegal immigrants, who often oppose increased legal immigration as well, claim that undocumented immigrants impose costs on the U.S. economy. The Center for Immigration Studies, a group that does not favor increased immigration, says it costs the U.S. economy $10.5 billion a year for health care and education for illegal immigrants, net of what those immigrants who are working pay in taxes. Another group, the Federation for American Immigration Reform, calculates that California alone pays more than $10 billion a year because it receives more illegal immigrants than any other state and has to educate their children in public schools. That latter figure, however, appears not to take account of the taxes that employed illegal immigrants pay, even though almost all are employed and do pay taxes. In most cases, too, they pay into a Social Security system from which they will never receive a benefit. The Social Security system acknowledges that it collects $7 billion a year that goes unclaimed—most of it thought to come from workers listed under false Social Security numbers.

The real oversight is that the positive contribution that undocumented immigrants make to the U.S. economy is seldom mentioned. A crude but logical estimate of illegal immigrants' overall contribution to the economy, based on assumptions of minimum wage work for, let us say, 7 million people—leaving children out of the equation—amounts to $98 billion annually. The same calculation for California, at its slightly higher state minimum wage, yields a total of roughly $41 billion. There is little doubt that undocumented immigrants offer benefits to the economies of California and the United States through their labor in fields and factories, meat-packing plants and restaurants, domestic and janitorial service. That said, however, one cannot be in favor of illegal immigration. It is unfair to the legal immigrant waiting in line; it induces illegal behavior in employers; and most of all, it is unjust to the illegal entrant, who remains vulnerable to exploitation throughout his or her life here.

So solutions must be found in reforms that regularize the status of those now working in the United States and somehow stem the tide of unlawful entrants. A path to citizenship is necessary for those who have made working lives here. That, after all, has been the nation's tradition, dating to the four hundred thousand European immigrants who came as indentured servants from 1630 to 1700 and stayed here to help found the United States of America.[10] Aspiring citizens have always had hurdles to clear, including tests of knowledge and health—and longer waits for full "papers" than are required today. So conditions may be imposed on former illegal aliens being brought out of the shadows. But respect and a path to full participation in American life must exist for hard-working people who have given their labor and their hope to the United States.

New People in a New Land

Meanwhile, a general accusation that Latino immigrants won't assimilate is a myth being fed not only by the populist xenophobia that has always been a part of American life, but by the writings of some professors at leading universities. For example, Harvard's Samuel P. Huntington suggested in his 2004 book *Who Are We?* that Latino immigration poses a threat to the cultural integrity of the United States. Fortunately, stories that counter such positions abound. And few are more abundant in lessons for Southern California and the entire nation than the story of the Hernandez family. It is a classic story of hard work and education bringing a family to the heights of our society within three generations. "I'm very proud of my family," said Rick Hernandez. "My grandfather on my father's side came to a copper mining town in Arizona, but my grandfather didn't work in the mines. He had some kind of administrator's position. The copper ran out so my father's family, five boys and four girls, left for Los Angeles where there was work during World War II. My mother's family came to Tucson and then also came here and settled in East Los Angeles. My mother and her three sisters became secretaries and bought the house they lived in for their mother. When they married they all lived within walking distance of each other." Hernandez smiles as he recalls his mother's devotion to education and her ambition. "My father dropped out of high school and joined the army in the Korean War. He came home and married my mother. She wanted him to become a lawyer but he went on to join the Los Angeles Police Department. He was one of those who achieved the rank of lieutenant like Tom Bradley [who became mayor of Los Angeles]."[11] The elder Hernandez later earned his high school diploma and an associate degree at East Los Angeles College.

It was because of Enrique "Hank" Hernandez Sr.'s Mexican family background that he received an assignment in 1968 to help the Mexican authorities prepare security for the upcoming Olympic Games in Mexico City. He went to Mexico to help train the police force, even as the Mexican Army battled student protestors—and at one point killed 267 and injured 1,000 more at a demonstration. It was also a year of demonstrations against the Vietnam War, of riots, and of killings—Martin Luther King Jr., Robert F. Kennedy—in the United States. Policeman Hernandez noticed that wealthy people in Mexico hired guards and lived behind walls. He thought that similar patterns of security consciousness would emerge in U.S. society. So when he retired from the police force in 1973, he founded Inter-Con. From the start, it was not a typical security firm, employing former police officers as bank guards and night watches. Hernandez devised a security system that combined electronic surveillance with guards and alarms. It helped Inter-Con win a contract from NASA at Edwards Air Force Base. In the 1980s, he successfully proposed the idea of training security guards to supplement the Marines in protecting U.S. embassies and government officials around the world. The business prospered because, as Hank Hernandez foresaw, needs for security grew.

Today, demands for security are greater than ever and have gone stratospheric since September 11, 2001. "Our service used to deal with middle managers, but after 9/11, security became a matter of which chief executives and boards of directors had to be sure. So, we were called into the front offices," says Rick Hernandez, who took Inter-Con's reins from his father in the 1980s. The elder Hernandez died in 2006 at age seventy-four. Rick Hernandez has extended the tradition of using advanced technology with skilled personnel to protect hospitals and athletic arenas, as well as corporate and government operations. He staffs Inter-Con with many former military officers. "We are the largest provider of hospital security and many other kinds of security in the nation," Hernandez says.

Inter-Con now has thirty thousand employees. It is a private company so Hernandez doesn't reveal revenue and profit information, but a firm with its scale of operations and importance easily has $2 billion in revenue annually. That would make it the largest Hispanic-owned firm in the nation, but its name appears on no lists of that kind. "We keep quiet about ourselves," Hernandez says. "We're a security firm after all. We protect clients' information and our own, and besides, my dad always said let your work speak for you." And the Hernandezes' work does speak: the company now operates around the globe, including in Mexico, where Inter-Con protects shipments from hijackers on remote mountain turnpikes. "We use satellite positioning, so we can follow all trucks going from Mexico City to the port of Vera Cruz," he says. "But if a truck is hijacked, we can immobilize it by remote signal and send our people to apprehend the criminal." Hernandez sees opportunity for his company in training police forces in developing countries, as Inter-Con has done in Mexico.

Now leader of one major company and director of other premier corporations and philanthropic organizations, Rick Hernandez quite simply *is* part of the American establishment. And he knows the context of his position, as well as that of others in Latino society. Asked by a midwestern businessman at a dinner in Los Angeles how he thought Mexican immigrants would fare in "American society," Hernandez calmly reminded the questioner that "Mexican families in California go back five or ten or more generations. The newest generations will work hard and achieve as have all the rest."

Latino Markets

And they have worked hard and achieved. The Selig Center for Economic Growth at the University of Georgia estimates the buying power of the Latino community in the United States today at nearly $862 billion, more than 6 percent of the nation's gross domestic product (figure 4.1).[12] The largest chunk of that buying power, setting the pace for all other markets, is more than $200 billion of buying power concentrated in Southern California. By 2012 that national purchasing power will exceed $1.2 trillion. Sheer purchasing power is not the only distinction of today's new immigrant populations. Their economic and educational progress is quicker than that of immigrant groups in former times. In

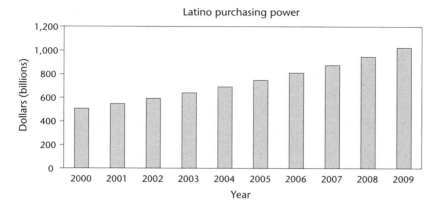

Figure 4.1. Statistics over a decade, showing rising purchasing power in the Latino community. Source: Author's calculations based on research from the Pew Hispanic Center, Selig Center for Economic Growth at the University of Georgia.

a 2006 study titled "Immigrants and Their Schooling," James P. Smith, senior economist at the RAND Corp., found that Mexican immigrants today attain greater levels of education across three generations than earlier comparably large immigrant groups.[13] In plain language, Latino grandchildren today go to college more than Irish and Italian grandchildren did in the nineteenth and early twentieth centuries.

That really shouldn't be surprising. The demand for skills is greater in today's economy, so more education is imperative. And Latino newcomers have more opportunities to move up in income and status than immigrants possessed in former times, when California and the United States were poorer. Working people in the past had less access to home mortgages or small loans for business and consumer purchases. By comparison, special small business departments of major banks have pursued Latino groups in recent years. Access to capital has made possible an abundant variety of immigrant-led small companies in Southern California (see Chapter 3). Chairman of City National Corp. Russell Goldsmith, a Los Angeles banker with ambitions to expand in the Latino market, estimates that there are 340,000 Latino-owned small to medium-sized companies in California, including 25,000 that take in more than $1 million in annual revenue. "That's a very attractive market," Goldsmith observes.[14] He's not alone in that judgment.

Three groups in Southern California have organized banks devoted to the Latino small business market. And elite, old family money is now joining prominent businesspeople in the Latino community to invest in their businesses. I tell here of banks being formed to serve the Latino community, of businesses that started out as ethnic specialties and grew to have influence across the nation, and of private equity funds in the tens of millions of dollars being formed to invest in Latino family businesses. I also tell of national organizations to promote good jobs for Latino youngsters at the highest levels of corporate finance. The momentum of this community is *very* powerful.

I begin with the banks, Promerica Bank, Americas United Bank, and the Banco del Tepeyac, because they are in a great American tradition. In 1850, Emigrant Savings Bank was organized in New York by Irish immigrants to serve Irish immigrants. In 1904, Amadeo Peter Giannini, the son of Italian immigrants, opened the Bank of Italy to make loans to Italian fishermen and small businesspeople in San Francisco. The Emigrant survives to this day, serving the five boroughs of New York City. Giannini's Bank of Italy changed its name to Bank of America in 1932 and today is one of America's largest financial institutions. The founders and investors of the three Latino banks are equally interesting and expressive of long-term developments in the U.S. economy and those of neighboring countries.

Promerica Bank was founded in 2006 by Maria Contreras-Sweet, who emigrated from Guadalajara, Mexico, with her parents when she was five years old and rose to become secretary of transportation, business, and housing in California's state government. Back in private life in 2005, she ran an investment company and raised $26 million to start Promerica "to teach small businesspeople in the Latino community to manage cash flow and to build a market plan," she told me. She feels that a bank specifically for the Latino community will be able to pay attention to the family spirit of small companies. "People want to build a business for the generations," Contreras-Sweet says. "A business owner will say to me, 'I want this for my two sons and my daughter; I want to fix it so they don't have to sell it.'" On the other hand, family businesses often sell or merge in response to changed circumstances or changing family dynamics. And that promises opportunity for banks like Promerica that understand Latino family sentiments. Contreras-Sweet's backers in Promerica include Hector and Norma Orci, advertising executives who came from Mexico City in the 1980s to found La Agencia de Orci & Asociados, one of the largest Spanish-language ad agencies in this country.[15]

The Orcis helped Honda to become the leading car in the Latino market for most of the past two decades because they understood the unspoken characteristics of the potential Latino customers. Norma Orci explained that the usual methods of U.S. car dealers, of urging customers to take test drives, hurt sales instead of helped in the Latino market. "For the immigrant customer, buying a car is a very big event, a family affair. But when the customer was given a test drive, he felt an obligation to buy the vehicle because the dealer had done him the favor of letting him drive," Orci said. "But that made the customer uncomfortable, with the result that they stopped going to the dealer and they did not buy the cars." What did the Orcis do differently? They took Honda into the Latino community as a sponsor of Little League baseball and other community activities. Then when Honda made a point of explaining to potential customers that there was no obligation, those customers tended to believe the company because of its involvement in the community. This story points to the kind of opportunity available in this new and growing market for those who understand it.

Among the banks, the backers of Banco del Tepeyac are intriguing because they include several dozen investors from Mexico who see opportunity in family companies in the United States that they do not recognize in their own country. The bank, which received its charter in March 2007, was formed by Emilio Sanchez-Santiago, a veteran executive on three continents for Citicorp, who is originally from Mexico. He raised $18 million from eighty investors in the United States and Mexico to open Tepeyac in Huntington Park, a heavily Latino city of sixty-two thousand in Los Angeles County. Huntington Park's main street is filled with businesses of shopkeepers and tradespeople. "I look at this market in terms of opportunity," Sanchez-Santiago told me. Hoping to compete with larger U.S. banks by getting close to individual customers, Tepeyac is going after small savings and checking account deposits of recent immigrants and their offspring. Thus its name, which is sacred to all Mexicans because it comes from the Hill of Tepeyac, a site outside Mexico City where a peasant named Juan Diego saw a vision of the Virgin Mary as Our Lady of Guadalupe. The Basilica of Our Lady of Guadalupe stands there today.

Sanchez-Santiago's bank is especially significant because it is bringing Mexican investors into the U.S. venture. The investors like the prospects for "family companies in Los Angeles," Jose Akle told me. Akle is the owner of a telecommunications company in Mexico and a Tepeyac investor. But no, he said, he cannot see investing in small companies in Mexico itself right now—"impossible." However, Akle believes that growing Latino companies in the United States could contribute to creditworthiness for small firms in Mexico. "We see this investment in Latino companies in Los Angeles as a first step," Akle said. He is hoping that sending money out of Mexico can provide a ricochet "first step" to help small businesses in Mexico, a country that does not have a tradition of helping entrepreneurs.[16]

Cuban Connection

Traditions are different among the Cuban population of Southern California, most of whom came here in the late 1950s after the Cuban Revolution. In a few decades, that community has founded many thriving businesses and in 2007 supported the formation of Americas United Bank. The bank is backed by a hefty $28.7 million of investment from six Southern California Cuban business families, along with three hundred other initial shareholders. "But don't stress the Cuban aspect," Gilbert Dalmau, a Cuban American, veteran banker, and bank president told me. "This bank is to serve the whole Hispanic community and all the other small business communities here." The real significance of the "Cuban aspect" is that it is younger members of Cuban business families who led the investment to organize the bank.[17]

How these families came to the United States is as good a story as how they built their businesses. Jorge Rodriguez, the chief financial and operations officer of Mercado Latino, Inc., is a good example. Jorge was born in Cuba, where his father was in the wholesale grocery business. In 1961, as fidel Castro's government was imposing Soviet-style changes on the economy, Jorge, then thirteen, his sister Angie, and brothers

Richard and Roberto left Cuba in a remarkable program called Operation Peter Pan (Operación Pedro Pan). Through a two-year collaboration between the Catholic Church in Cuba and in Florida, U.S. government authorities, and generous volunteers in both countries, fourteen thousand children were sent out of Cuba between 1960 and 1962 before Castro's government caught on. The children went to temporary foster homes in Miami, where they filed applications for visas so their parents could follow to the United States. The program lasted long enough to get Jorge's father and mother out of Cuba. Immediately the family was sent on to the Los Angeles area because there were more Cubans in Miami than jobs to occupy them. "We went to Long Beach where there was a house for us to stay in and my dad had a job to go to in the morning," Jorge recalled.

His father, Graciliano Rodriguez, went to work waiting tables in a private club and doing janitorial work. But soon, the elder Rodriguez found a way to work for himself in food distribution. He opened a store in the Los Angeles produce market dealing in the kinds of beans, rice, and special vegetables that people from Mexico and Central America favored. That was the foundation of Mercado Latino, which today has operations in eleven western states; more than one hundred trucks plying the roads from Washington State to Texas; two hundred to four hundred employees, depending on seasonal needs; and more than $120 million in annual revenue. Among other customers, Mercado supplies specialty products to Wal-Mart Stores, the nation's largest retailer. Mercado Latino even sends its Mexican-style products into Mexico through the H. E. Butt Grocery Co. (H-E-B), a San Antonio, Texas, supermarket chain that has stores in Monterrey, Mexico. Perhaps in another time, the Rodriguezes would have been able to start a small family grocery, a mom-and-pop *tienda* in a Latino neighborhood. But in today's America, the family company can go far beyond that because of the growing size of the Hispanic market in all parts of the nation, particularly the West, and because of the sophistication of food distribution and finance in the economy.

Mercado is far from a unique example of Cuban success. C&F Foods Inc., based in Industry, California, was founded in 1975 by Cuban émigré Jose Fernandez. It is run today by his grandson Luis Faura and has become one of the country's largest processors and distributors of beans—pinto, black, and red beans and other varieties central to the Latin American diet. Beans have grown in popularity with rising recognition among U.S. consumers of their high-fiber, high-protein health attributes and with the growth of Latino populations in all parts of the country. "We have a distribution center in North Carolina that supplies the Southeast," Faura said. "It never was a big market before, but now there are people from South America and Mexico and El Salvador in Atlanta and Raleigh and everywhere." C&F Foods, meanwhile, has grown to 285 employees and well over $100 million in annual revenue by looking beyond ethnic markets to broader trends among consumers. It saw the increasing demand for organic produce in the United States and invested to supply it. "It's a good business and the profit is there, but you have to be ready to bear the cost of getting into it," Faura says. To qualify as an organic food supplier, he explains, a company needs to invest in more costly fertilizers and machinery for milling and packing the beans. When the organic food phenomenon began in 2000 or so, "we debated whether it was a fad or a trend. It took almost $8 million of investment. But we decided to go for it," Faura recalls. "And now we have that 'first-mover' advantage." Faura is one of the founding investors in Americas United Bank, as are some younger members of the Gaviña family, organizers of F. Gaviña & Sons. The company makes specialty coffee that its Cuban refugee founders first aimed at Latin tastes but now distribute to the U.S. mass market. Gaviña supplies coffee to McDonald's throughout the western states and also sells in supermarkets.

Of course, one advantage the Cuban émigrés had before coming to the United States is that they owned and ran family businesses back in Cuba. The great majority of Mexican immigrants in this and previous generations have not had experience in business of any kind. That is because Mexico's economy offers almost no access to capital for small businesses. Indeed, one of the principal sources of support for people in Mexican villages are the remittances that family members who have gone to the United States send back to Mexico. In 2007, those remittances totaled more than $24 billion, according to the Bank of Mexico, the country's central bank, which reported that remittances in 2008 were running hundreds of millions of dollars lower because of the slowdown in the U.S. economy.[18] Poor people in the mountains of Mexico seeing such remittances must believe, as others have done for two centuries, that the "streets are paved with gold" in the United States. Small wonder that the poor of Mexico try to get here by any means possible—legal or illegal. Mexico's economy remains stifled by a large government structure that limits opportunity for entrepreneurial business. Key segments of industry, telecommunications, and energy operate under private or government monopolies. Thus, Mexico's gross domestic product of $893.4 billion is less than that of Southern California—despite the fact that Mexico's population is 106 million and Southern California has one-fifth that many people.[19]

Pobre México

What can be done to improve Mexico's economy? The same thing many other countries have done to improve the productivity of their people, their human capital. If Mexico reformed its economy and developed opportunities for its people, the flow of those going north in hopes of a better life for themselves and their children would lessen. Japan, Israel, and Ireland are often held up as examples of countries with few natural resources but productive human capital that has made them rich in the information age. Ireland is a particularly good example, since as late as fifty years ago it was still the poorest country in Europe and still sent millions of poor people to the United States in a tradition spanning more than one hundred years. My own mother and father were part of that long chain of immigrants from Ireland, each coming during the 1920s with only six years of education, which prepared them for menial jobs in warehouses and domestic service. Yet they worked and made lives in a new land and sent remittances back to brothers and sisters in the land from which they had come.

But all has changed for Ireland now, as it can for Mexico. Today, Ireland is one of the richest countries in Europe,[20] on a per capita basis, partly because it became a member of the European Community in 1973 and thereby gained access to an enormous market for its farms and industries. Also, it gained sizable investments from U.S. companies drawn by that very access to Europe and by the supply of educated employees that Ireland raised with requirements that its young people do extra study of math, science, and languages. Now, the Irish people, classic poor immigrants for 150 years, are no longer leaving their homeland. Mexico has a similar opportunity. The North American Free Trade Agreement links it to the United States and Canada and potentially can bring it abundant investment. But it must modernize its political and economic institutions, and it must do a better job of educating its young people. (Educating young people is as much a challenge for Los Angeles and all of Southern California, as we shall see in Chapter 8.) Time will tell whether it will meet this challenge and erase forever the sad lament of its nineteenth-century president Porfirio Díaz, who is credited with saying, "Pobre México! Tan lejos de Dios, y tan cerca de los Estados Unidos!" (Poor Mexico! So far from God and so close to the United States!).

Meanwhile, of course, American streets were never paved with gold and are not today. Despite the entrepreneurs and thriving small businesses mentioned above, many immigrants from Latin America are poor and struggling as migrant farmworkers in California and other states, menial laborers, and domestic servants in suburban neighborhoods. Yet neither should arguments about poor, unskilled immigrants obscure the fact that for the most part, Latino immigrants work for more than a minimum wage. For example, at Quatrine Custom Furniture, a Los Angeles–area furniture company, hourly pay is $10 per hour plus health benefits for the employee. For some employees with great skills, pay goes to $13 an hour and above. And by paying an additional premium, employees can get health benefits extended to their families. "You have to pay good people to keep them," says owner Gina Quatrine.[21] This returns us to the central theme of this chapter, that America's Latino story today is really one of assimilation and new energy for the U.S. economy and its future. I close this chapter with three outstanding examples that illustrate the powerful spirit that drives Latino community leaders today to build for the future.

Double Bottom Lines

Daniel D. Villanueva is a founder of Spanish-language media, an investor in Latino family businesses, and a leader of the New America Alliance, which is working for the educational and economic advancement of Latino young people.[22] Villanueva (shown in Figure 4.2) grew up in New Mexico of immigrant parents and became a professional football player, earning good money as place kicker for the Dallas Cowboys and Los Angeles Rams. When he retired from the game in 1968, he invested his earnings in one of the first Spanish-language television stations in the Los Angeles area, KMEX, Channel 34. "We went door to door asking if people wanted to buy a converter box to bring in UHF transmission," Villanueva recalled, "because those channels weren't yet made standard for TV sets by FCC [Federal Communications Commission] regulations." Then in the 1970s, Villanueva joined similar startup stations in Miami, Phoenix, and San Antonio, setting up the Spanish International Network with assistance and investment from Mexico's Televisa network and its owners the Azcárraga family. But in 1986, the FCC forced the sale of Spanish International because the Azcárragas' holding was greater than 20 percent and was thus in violation of U.S. legal restrictions on foreign ownership. The fledgling network was sold at that time to Hallmark Cards and the first Chicago Bank for $301 million. Villanueva's share of the proceeds laid the foundation of his fortune, which is estimated today in the $100 million range.

Figure 4.2. Father and son, Daniel D. Villanueva and Daniel L. Villanueva, along with Gabrielle Greene, partners in the Rustic Canyon/Fontis Partners (RC/Fontis) investment firm. Photo by Christine Carter Conway.

Villanueva stayed three years with the Hallmark-owned company, which struggled in what was then a new business. Ultimately, the Spanish-language service, which was renamed Univision, sold in 1992 to private investors in Los Angeles, who ran it for fourteen years and then sold it in a highly publicized bidding contest in 2006 for $13 billion. This enormous rise in value over the decade and a half attests to the growth and attractiveness of Latino markets in the United States. "Univision does better than the major television networks in L.A. and other big cities today," Villanueva points out. After selling his stake in the television business, Villanueva cofounded an investment company named Bastion Capital, which backed ventures in media, including a chain of Spanish-language radio stations owned by Tom Castro, a California-born, Harvard-trained entrepreneur. Today, Castro's company, Border Media Partners, owns thirty-five radio stations in Texas, where family-owned country and popular music stations are selling out to buyers who can serve the salsa and ranchera music popular with immigrants. Thirteen of Castro's stations now broadcast in a combination of English and Spanish, reflecting changing audience dynamics.

But even as Villanueva grew richer on opportunities for Bastion, which made investments in the tens of millions of dollars, he had a new vision. "I wanted to organize a venture capital fund for small Latino-owned businesses," he says. "My instincts told me that a fund able to invest in the $5 million to $15 million range would do the most good and help Latino entrepreneurs and family businesses." So with his son Daniel L. Villanueva, a Stanford graduate who had trained in the advertising business, Villanueva organized Fontis Ventures in 2004 to invest small sums in companies that need capital as founders want to retire and hand the company reins over to their offspring, or simply sell and cash out. "The new generation is university trained as opposed to the founders, who were not trained," says Daniel Jr. "We help family companies move beyond their local bank financing." Then in 2005, the Villanuevas found a partner for Fontis in Rustic Canyon Partners, a firm that invests for the Chandler family, a premier name in old California money. Throughout the twentieth century, the Chandler family, owners of the *Los Angeles Times*, led the expansion of Southern California. Succeeding generations of the family fostered the growth of the port at San

Pedro, the acquisition of water from the Sierra Nevada, and the founding of economic, educational, and cultural institutions. The Chandlers sold the newspaper just as the twenty-first century dawned, and with part of the proceeds the family's money manager has joined the Villanuevas in Rustic Canyon/Fontis Partners (RC/Fontis), raising $80 million to invest in Latino family companies.

And public money in the form of the California Public Employees' Retirement System, or CalPERS, has joined them as investors looking for a "double bottom line." To explain, RC/Fontis, like all venture and private equity firms, looks for returns on investment of 20 percent to 30 percent a year over five years. Pension funds and trusts invest with firms like RC/Fontis to obtain returns that help them meet their long-term obligations and, at the same time, benefit businesses and people in minority communities—a "double bottom line." Similarly, the Villanuevas and other Latino businesspeople have a broad community perspective on their success in U.S. society. In 2001, in Santa Fe, New Mexico, they formed the New America Alliance. Danny Villanueva Sr. recalls: "We wanted to do something to promote opportunities for Latin American young people, but we didn't want to interfere with other organizations or take government money. So we went around the room and raised $1 million in fifteen minutes for the New America Alliance, which has two purposes, education and philanthropy." The alliance takes a practical approach to its programs. It holds a convention on Wall Street every October and "brings pressure on Wall Street to increase capital access for Latinos and to hire Latino MBAs in their financial companies," says Norma Orci. "We have had some success."[23]

Home and Hearth

Another outstanding Latino leader is Henry Cisneros. The son of immigrants to San Antonio, Texas, Cisneros graduated from Texas A&M University, became mayor of San Antonio, and then became secretary of housing and urban development during the Clinton administration. After his service in Washington, D.C., he founded CityView, one of the country's largest companies involved in inner-city home building. The company, backed by a $500 million revolving fund from CalPERS, has built six thousand homes in California and major cities across the nation, including Chicago, Detroit, and Denver. Cisneros's company specializes in building only affordable housing. "I call it work force housing," Cisneros says, "because it is meant for the moderate-income working people that are the heart of every community."[24] CityView gears the cost of its houses to a price that equals one and one-half times the median income for a local community. Unfortunately, Cisneros's projects suffered in the 2008 subprime crisis and decline in house prices. Cisneros in a *New York Times* article expressed regret that he did not see the crisis coming. Still, developers, investors, and prominent individuals continue to find that investment in urban areas is a way of doing good while doing well.

Oscar De La Hoya, the championship boxer, is an emblematic character in every immigrant group's saga. His tale is an updated version of the scrappy kid from a poor neighborhood who fights his way to the top. De La Hoya, who is unmarked and handsome after 266 amateur and professional fights, and not yet retired at age thirty-five, is also a notably successful businessman who owns an office building in downtown Los Angeles worth an estimated $32 million. He also owns a fight-promoting business, Spanish-language media properties, and other endeavors. And he has a sense of mission, so he has entered a $100 million partnership to "revitalize Latino neighborhoods by building nice homes that are affordable for people who work in the area, teachers, nurses, fire and police."[25] De La Hoya, who acquired the nickname of Golden Boy after winning championships in six weight divisions in professional boxing, calls his new company Golden Boy Partners. His coinvestor and partner is one of Southern California's smartest real estate investors, John Long, who has bought and sold more than $6 billion in commercial real estate during a thirty-year career (see Chapter 5 for more on Long).

Long was seven years old when he moved from China with his parents to Los Angeles in 1954. Like De La Hoya, he grew up in a poor neighborhood where immigrant families had no chance to own their homes because mortgages were not available for low-income people. Today, mortgages are available, and De La Hoya describes his joint venture with Long, which began in 2006 with a project to build 107 townhouses on the site of a shuttered industrial facility in south Los Angeles County, this way: "Obviously, we go into business to make money, but at the same time we want to help families." The project began construction in 2008.

De La Hoya was training for yet another championship fight in early 2007 when I interviewed him. Also, he was writing a book. "I want to write about the contribution of Latinos to the future of America," he said. As Rick Hernandez puts it, "we are lucky to be here. . . . The energy of people coming here makes this . . . The center of gravity of the world economy." It is fitting that De La Hoya is teaming with Long because the Chinese are the second largest immigrant group affecting the role of Southern California in the world economy. Chinese Americans, though fewer in number than Latinos, have created bridges to China in business and trade and in turn bridges to the United States in business philosophy and vision. The next chapter tells of Southern California's Chinese American businesspeople and of their intriguing mixture of a Chinese way and an American way, which could influence the U.S. economy and outlook for years to come.

Bridges to China

> Southern California is the real connecting spot between Asia
> and North America because we embrace people. This is the
> first place in history where the collective minority population
> becomes the majority.
>
> Donald Tang,
> immigrant from China, investment banker,
> president of the Asia Society of Southern California

CHINESE IMMIGRANTS to Southern California define America's current opening to Asia, economically, historically, and philosophically. In trade, the region is the recipient of $159 billion worth of goods from China. It is those U.S. imports that generate much of China's $1.8 trillion in foreign exchange reserves and therefore the $922 billion that China invests in U.S. Treasury bonds and financial instruments.[1] That's not a distant, abstract connection. Partly because of China's investment in those Treasury bonds, interest rates remained low in recent years, and U.S. housing and consumer markets, for the most part, have been vibrant. That tidy, symbiotic relationship is losing force in 2008 with a retreat of U.S. housing and consumer markets. But the China connection isn't going away; indeed, it is coming closer.

Lately, the region has also become a destination for China's brick and mortar investments. Chinese companies are buying warehouse properties, setting up operations, and seeking partnerships and alliances in Southern

California. Such Chinese investment in the region may total $5 billion, which is not a lot, but local financiers expect investments to rise.[2]

Still, investment from China is relatively minor compared with the size and success of businesses created by Chinese Americans in Southern California. Three leading banking companies in the region's Chinese community, for example, have more than $20 billion in assets among them and operations in China and Vietnam as well as New York and Texas.[3] As entrepreneurs in high technology or as global financiers, as makers of toys and garments or as leaders in real estate and food processing, Chinese Americans are succeeding in a whole gamut of trades and industry. Indeed, after two centuries of Chinese immigration, two generations of new immigrants from the area known as Greater China (the territories of the People's Republic of China, including Hong Kong, and the Republic of China, including Taiwan) have brought Chinese communities out of traditional Chinatowns and into the American mainstream while at the same time building bridges back to China in the form of investments and demonstrations of "Yankee" ingenuity and enterprise.

These new Americans also have ambitions beyond riches: to spread knowledge of China's culture in the United States and to produce a fresh synthesis of American dynamism with Confucian wisdom. For instance, Chinese Americans are introducing Chinese modern art to American galleries. And in partnership with American institutions, they have raised $18 million to build a Chinese Garden on the grounds of the Huntington Library in Pasadena, a cultural landmark that is the bequest of the Huntington family, earlier builders of California (see Figure 5.1).

Chinese Americans have come to prominence since passage of the Immigration Act of 1965 opened the way finally for Asian people to contribute their talents to the United States. This chapter presents stories of the new Chinese Americans, setting them against a backdrop of the long history of prejudice and suffering that Chinese people have endured in this country. The stories' central characters are Chinese American businesspeople, but the chapter's underlying theme explains this new time in which the massive U.S. economy is linked in a mutually beneficial relationship with the developing economy of China. Among other factors, that relationship is dictated by historic demographics: according

Figure 5.1. View of a lake and pagoda in the Chinese Garden at the Huntington Library in Pasadena. The garden was built largely with donations from the Chinese American community. Reproduced by permission of the Huntington Library, Art Collections and Botanical Gardens.

to economist Kenneth Courtis, two-thirds of the world's young people, those between the teen years and age forty, live today in Asia.[4] Courtis, a scholar and fluent speaker of both Japanese and Mandarin Chinese, headed Asian research first for Deutsche Bank and then for Goldman Sachs. In 2005, he founded the investment fund Next Capital Partners. His view today is that the economic rise we see in Asia is part of a much broader shift in world culture. "What we are seeing is nothing less than an Asian Renaissance, a cultural, economic, political reawakening not only in China but in India, Korea, Indonesia, Malaysia, all the other countries of Asia," Courtis said at a meeting of the Asia Society in Los Angeles in 2008.

That makes Southern California's ties across the Pacific Rim all the more valuable. Such connections have brought Asian students and scholars to this region's universities. These students and professors in turn have pioneered developments in biotechnology, nanotechnology, and computer science. As a consequence, Asian graduates have donated generously and served as trustees of the universities. Their business acumen has opened opportunities for Southern California businesses in China and brought investment from that country to this region.

Donald Tang exemplifies the energy and vision of Chinese America. The son of college professors in Shanghai, Tang came to the United States in 1982 at age eighteen. Having studied chemical engineering at the East China Institute of Technology, where his mother taught, Tang earned a bachelor's of science degree in chemical engineering from California State Polytechnic University in Pomona four years after arriving here. He went to work in finance, for Lehman Brothers, for Merrill Lynch, and then for Bear Stearns, the investment bank. Bear Stearns sent him to Hong Kong as head of Asian operations for six years and ultimately made him vice chairman. Bear Stearns was purchased by J. P. Morgan Chase in the financial crisis of 2008. Tang, who has extensive business relationships in Asia, left the bank in October 2008 to form his own global financial services firm.[5]

Promoting Knowledge

Tang also has pursued missions beyond business. He revived the Asia Society in Los Angeles and has brought senior officials of China's government to speak at conferences here. He has promoted conferences to study the Indian and Korean economies as well as that of China. He has also reached out to the African American community in South Los Angeles, introducing black community leaders to Chinese officials and scholars proposing economic education and investment in poor neighborhoods. And he introduced U.S. labor leaders, including Andy Stern, the influential head of the Service Employees International Union, to Chinese labor leaders. These introductions contributed to some labor agreements in China. His aim, Tang explains, is to foster knowledge and acceptance of the global economy, particularly China and Asia's rising role in it. "Those who benefit from globalization are those who are prepared educationally and mentally," Tang says. "And those who are not prepared see globalization as a threat, and that kind of fear can cause a collision. So I spend time with different communities to explain to them that like it or not the global economy is here and we can benefit by having more people in it." By "collision" he is referring to past instances of anti-

Asian violence in poor neighborhoods directed at Korean storeowners and also historic violence against Chinese American merchants. Tang shrugs when reminded of past prejudice. "America is the most open-minded society," he says. "The fact that we continue to progress is the cornerstone of America; we always come through."

Tang works for collaboration among Southern California's many diverse groups so that the region may fulfill a destiny of becoming the capital city of the global economy. "We have a shot at attracting headquarters of international business operations from Japan, Korea, Singapore, India, and China," he says. "We can make this a special economic zone in the world. We have to shout that this is the place to do it together." The urgency of his rhetoric reflects the fact that Tang and others in finance see a tide of investment from China building up. The Chinese companies that have offices in Southern California so far are only a vanguard of what is to come. "In the next five years, banks in Southern California will see great flows of deposits and investments coming from China," says Robert Sweeney, president of Far East National Bank, a three-decades-old Los Angeles institution that is a subsidiary of Bank Sinopac of Taiwan.[6]

The investors will be seeking a greater piece of the action. As explained in Chapter 1, Chinese manufacturers of goods for the U.S. market reap 20 percent or less of the value of any product. The lion's share of revenue and profit goes to those who transport the goods from China, pick them up at dockside in Los Angeles and Long Beach, distribute them throughout the United States, and sell them at retail. That's not to mention designers and marketers who contribute the original brainwork for the products. Some Chinese companies saw years ago that bringing operations closer to their ultimate customers spelled smart business. For example, Jiangsu Tongda Aerosol Co., a company that manufactures household products in Changzhou, China, set up an operation called Oscar Home Care in Ontario, California, six years ago to sell air fresheners at discount store chains in the United States. "We saw air fresheners as products we could ship at low cost to America," says Junwu Liu, the chairman of Tongda and the president of Oscar Home Care.[7] Selling fresheners through Dollar General Stores and other chains has grown to a business worth $6 million in annual sales. So Liu is looking for more products to push through Tongda's U.S. distribution network.

Anticipating more Asian companies coming to Southern California, Jason Chung, a Chinese immigrant working at first California Equity Group, a finance company in Pasadena, is building a $100 million business center in Santa Ana for Chinese industrial companies coming to set up operations in Southern California. "We can help them get up to value in branding, promotion, recruiting and finance," Chung says. He expects his own financing to come from China and from investment funds in the United States.[8]

This prosperous and expanding Sino-American business universe points to the way of the future for Southern California and the U.S. economy. Yet it is so recent as to appear inconstant and fleeting. So we need to reflect on history to understand how much Chinese people contributed to the development of California and how they were despised and excluded until a relatively short time ago. Then we can see with more confidence how the positive trends of today reflect openness to changes in the global economy that, as Donald Tang says, are here "like it or not."

Fruit and Laundries

Chinese immigrants first came in significant numbers to California in 1849, to what they called the Gold Mountain. They joined in mining for gold—with only a few finding much—and then were enlisted to build the Central Pacific Railroad. The California-to-Utah portion of the transcontinental railroad started in 1863 and finished in 1869. After that, came a less remembered achievement. Chinese laborers transformed California agriculture during the 1870s when they showed growers how to drain marshes, construct irrigation canals, and grow crops of fruit. They had brought knowledge of such agriculture from China's Yellow River region. For these contributions, they were not thanked but excluded. Little more than three decades after they came to America, Chinese laborers were barred from further immigration when Congress passed the Chinese Exclusion Act in 1882. In California, a law called the Geary Act required every Chinese person to openly wear identification tags and to constantly face the possibility of deportation on trumped-up grounds.

Agitation by white laborers against Chinese workers, who were paid less than white workers—and who were accused of working far less than they actually did—was behind the exclusion laws. San Francisco was a center of anti-Chinese labor protests, one result of which was to force Chinese men into self-employment; they started restaurants, stores, and especially laundries. In fact, the Chinese laundryman was an American phenomenon, as historian Ronald Takaki points out. In China, women did the washing, not men. But in America, laundry work became a business that a man could start with a low capital investment and without speaking much English.[9]

Stupid jokes about Chinese laundrymen mispronouncing English arose during those early days, but the exclusion laws were no joke. They were extended and tightened in succeeding decades, nationally and at state levels, for Chinese American people. Repeal of the laws did not come until 1943 when America needed Chinese American soldiers for battle and Chinese American women to work in defense plants. Indeed, even after they were called to serve in war and industry, Chinese Americans still could not own land in California until a state law was finally repealed in 1956.[10]

But things began to change during the 1960s, particularly after the 1965 immigration law opened the United States to people from all countries. "Until then there were really very few Chinese people here even in Los Angeles," says Gareth Chang, who immigrated with his parents from Hong Kong in 1960, studied physics and math at California State University, Fullerton—and later earned a master's of business administration (MBA) from Pepperdine University—and went on to become a major executive in the aerospace and high-tech industries while teaching part time at Beijing's Tsinghua University.[11] Emerging economies of Hong Kong, Taiwan, and Singapore also brought major changes to Southern California during the 1960s. Greater China sent merchandise and people to the United States, who set up banks and opened factories that made parts for products that would later be put together on the other side of the Pacific. Mainland China still was shrouded in the decaying rule of Mao Tse-tung, but the potential was there for the tremendous revival that would change the world—and Southern California—during the 1990s.

Banking Pioneers

The saga of two immigrant bankers, the institutions they built, and some of their notable customers illustrates the remarkable story of how a new economy is being constructed through bridges to China and new passages to America. Henry Hwang was an immigrant from Shanghai via Taiwan whose first job in Los Angeles was managing a laundry. While doing that, he also studied accounting at the University of Southern California and in 1960 opened a practice in the San Gabriel Valley, an area of Los Angeles County that was becoming home to thousands of immigrants from Hong Kong, Taiwan, and China. Money was beginning to flow into the area as immigrant business owners engaged in two-way trade with relatives and partners in their homelands. Seeing a good thing, Hwang opened Far East National Bank in 1974, the first Chinese-owned, nationally chartered bank in the United States.[12] He was becoming a successful businessman, yet when he tried to buy a house in the posh San Marino area of Pasadena, realtors refused to sell to an Asian. (Today, San Marino has a large Asian population.) But Hwang was irrepressible by nature. He kept his bank open evenings and Saturdays for the benefit of his small business customers. He called America "this land of opportunity" to every prospect and listener and emblazoned the bank's annual reports with the slogan "Fulfilling the American Dream." He helped translate the U.S. Constitution into Chinese for the benefit of his immigrant clientele and friends. A man with a love of music and a strong baritone voice, he also translated and sang Handel oratorios at the church he and his family attended.

Hwang became interested in politics, contributing heavily to the 1980 campaign of Ronald Reagan for president and winning an appointment on a White House advisory commission on trade. But his contributions and close ties to Los Angeles mayor Tom Bradley resulted in a scandal about making improper payments to the mayor and a grand jury investigation. Hwang was found innocent of wrongdoing.

Despite all his work and contributions, banker Hwang had little or no relation to the ruling caste of business leadership in Los Angeles, whether old money in places like Pasadena or show business money in Beverly Hills. This rankled Hwang all his days (he died of cancer at age seventy-seven in 2005). But in business, he had the last laugh as history brought opportunity to him. He opened offices of Far East National in Beijing as the new Chinese economy emerged and helped to finance hotels and office buildings in his once native land. He shepherded early Chinese investments in warehouses and other industrial buildings in the Los Angeles area. His bank grew to ten branches and $500 million in assets. He told me in 1996 that Chinese investors were asking his bank to find prospects for them in "warehouses and commercial and industrial property." Hwang was ahead of his time in understanding that Chinese companies wanted to get more involved in the U.S. economy. In fact, Hwang had a vision of Far East as a conduit for China investments when he sold the bank in 1997 for $94 million to Taiwan's Bank SinoPac, a company run by Paul Lo, an old friend who had served as an officer of Citicorp in Los Angeles. Hwang and Lo thought alike about the possibilities of Chinese investment, but their vision did not come to pass for years because of difficulties in China's banking system and the concerns of U.S. bank regulators. Hwang, disillusioned at the slow pace of change, left Far East and moved his allegiance and many of his old employees over to rival East West Bank, of Los Angeles, which was being built into a major institution by an immigrant from Hong Kong named Dominic Ng. To Henry Hwang, who had struggled and prospered, Ng and others represented a new day. "There are great opportunities for Chinese in America now," Hwang said in 2003. "I tell Dominic to really go after them."

Advantage to Being Chinese

Dominic Ng, who had pioneered a practice serving the Chinese business community in Los Angeles for the Deloitte & Touche firm, was a young accountant when an Indonesian Chinese family named Nursalim recruited him in 1991 to lead the East West loan company they were buying for $40 million. Ng (shown in Figure 5.2) had moved to Texas from Hong Kong a dozen years earlier to study at the University of Houston, where his high marks attracted major accounting firms. They offered him jobs and, more important, helped him obtain a resident alien "green card" that allowed him to stay and work in the United States. (Ng wryly recalled the struggle to get that green card many years later as "proof that any immigrant who gets to stay in the United States has the energy and determination to survive an ordeal.") He moved to Los Angeles in 1986, when his parents immigrated to the United States, and continued working in accounting. "Here, it was an advantage to be Chinese," Ng says, "because you could relate to an expanding business community."[13]

From the start, Ng worked to convert East West from a savings and loan institution to a commercial bank. He understood that he was catering to an entrepreneurial business community, not simply a clientele of immigrants seeking mortgages from a bank that spoke their language. "These people did not come all the way here from Asia to work for a salary," Ng says. "Even if they came here to get engineering degrees and had good jobs at TRW and other aerospace companies, they were not satisfied. They wanted to own their own business. And that is why I wanted them as customers—they wanted to borrow money, they wanted to expand their business. They weren't thinking of retirement plans, they were planning new adventures." Clearly, Ng was early to see the new

Figure 5.2. Dominic Ng, chairman of East West Bank and leader in the Chinese business and civic community. Photo by Christine Carter Conway.

economy of Southern California as one led by small to medium-sized companies, even as most of the region sank into recession during the early 1990s because of cutbacks by aerospace-defense giants.

Ng proved to be entrepreneurial himself in 1998 as the Asian financial crisis hit the Nursalims, the owners of East West. The family told Ng to sell the bank to raise capital. But Ng didn't seek a buyer in a larger bank. Instead, he and his chief financial officer, Julia Gouw, also an immigrant to Los Angeles, decided to buy the bank themselves by offering large investing institutions access to the bank's enterprising customers. "We traveled for three weeks, not only to New York but to Boston, Philadelphia, Chicago, Dallas," Ng recalls. And at each presentation their trump cards were the same: "We put up $1 million each of our own money and so told these institutions that we were putting our whole net worth on the line." Impressed, 150 of the top financial institutions in the United States—including Merrill Lynch, Oppenheimer Funds, Wellington Management, and J. P. Morgan—agreed to invest more than $230 million along with Ng, Gouw, and associates to buy East West from the Nursalim family.

The investment has proved golden so far. By 2007, the bank had grown to an institution with $11.6 billion in assets, more than twelve hundred employees, and seventy-two branches in California, a new one in Hong Kong, and ambitions to open more offices in China and Vietnam. The major investment houses have a good profit and something more: an entree to a community of extremely active business customers. "We are now the largest Chinese bank in the United States," Ng told me proudly in 2006. "But we have become more than an ethnic bank. Fully 50 percent of our commercial banking business is non-Asian in clients or purpose. We are the largest Armenian bank and the largest bank for Persian business." He paused and then added, "on Asian business we offer special value. We are building a financial bridge to China for these small companies. That's what we want to always be."

Deals across the Sea

East West has backed numerous companies in its dealings across the Pacific, from quite small businesses to complex developments that form the base of innovative companies and great fortunes. Two of East West's clients in particular illustrate the changing realities and relationships of the Chinese and U.S. economies. The first is America Chung Nam, Inc., and its owner and organizer Yan Cheung. Cheung was a young female accountant in Hong Kong in the 1980s when she started buying scrap paper from the United States to feed China's growing need for boxes, writing paper, newsprint, and other products. In effect, she was connecting the American passion for recycling with the requirements of an industrializing country. Cheung moved to the United States in 1990 and set up her company in the City of Industry, a community east of Los Angeles that is filled with entrepreneurial firms. Soon Cheung was shipping two hundred thousand containers of waste cardboard and newspaper annually to China through the ports of Los Angeles and Long Beach. The waste is remade into corrugated boxes, which then are often filled with merchandise for shipment back to the United States. Eventually, the boxes become raw material once again for America Chung Nam.[14]

But then Cheung went further. She built Nine Dragons Paper Mill in Dongguan, China, near Hong Kong. She became not only the largest paper maker in China but one of its richest women when Nine Dragons sold stock on the Hong Kong Exchange in 2006. A fascinating footnote to the story is that she is the daughter of a military officer who was sent to prison as a counterrevolutionary during China's brutal Cultural Revolution in the 1960s and was released only in 1978, when Deng Xiaoping opened up the economy. Cheung, who lives these days in Hong Kong or Los Angeles, now has a second paper mill near Shanghai and a company with more than $1 billion in annual revenue. The bridge between China and Southern California is becoming a four-lane highway.

The truth of this statement is even clearer in a second example of an East West client. Roger Wang's story combines new opportunity in China and the American way of life and business. Wang came to the United States from Taiwan in 1971 to earn an MBA from Southeastern Louisiana University and then journeyed to Los Angeles, where he worked as a manager of a Thrifty drugstore. "There was not much I could use from my M.B.A. courses, but I learned stockroom organizing and inventory and how to merchandise to customers," Wang told me. That knowledge came in handy two years later when he started a retail operation selling convertible sofas to the Chinese immigrant community in the San Gabriel Valley. He became a U.S. citizen in 1978 and in the following decade succeeded in selling insurance and developing condominium apartments and small commercial buildings. Doing well enough, Wang was able to own a home in posh Beverly Hills and send his two daughters to private schools in the Los Angeles area.[15]

But when the Southern California economy went into decline during the early 1990s, Wang went to Nanjing, China, to visit friends and survey business possibilities. There he was commissioned to build a sixty-story office building—an opportunity that brought great challenge to his business and his life. Wang recalls that the idea of a sixty-story building sounded challenging but that the mayor of Nanjing, a city of 5 million on the Yangtze River, promised that the state-owned Industrial and Commercial Bank of China would provide the equivalent of $100 million in financing. "So I consulted with architects here in America and invested $4 million of my own money and started the project," he says. Building in China demanded fresh approaches in the early 1990s. The building standards were defined by Russian codes dating to 1945. "Human labor was so cheap that we didn't need to use machinery to dig the foundation," Wang says. However, the laborers had never worked on a building site or any kind of industrial project. So Wang had to "write out detailed descriptions of their tasks every day. I explained the purpose of the work and the concept of the building. It was like my days at Thrifty Drug," he says. "To make it work, you have to be a leader and an educator and an enforcer."

But then in 1993, the central government in Beijing, fearing inflation from a surge of building projects around the country, decreed a halt to bank loans for construction. Wang's bank partner quit the joint venture and pulled out all of its investments, leaving Wang "short $96 million of the funds needed." So he subdivided the building, which existed only in plans and blueprints, selling some space to local customers and banks. He also put in more of his own money and hung on, persuading suppliers to stick with the project on the promise of future payoff. Dominic Ng, Wang's friend and banker for ventures overseas as well as in California, recalls the time: "It was very hard. Roger stuck it out there while his wife and daughters were here in Beverly Hills."

Yet by 1995, six stories of the building were completed. And then Wang hit upon the idea of opening a department store in those floors while construction continued above them. He stocked the store with merchandise on concession—when the items sold, he could pay the suppliers. The store was a success, and cash flow from retailing operations helped finance the further construction of the building. The sixty-story skyscraper was completed in 1997, but by then, the department stores had taken on a life of their own. Success in Nanjing spawned new stores in other locations, including Xi'an and Suzhou. In 2005, the chain, which Wang named Golden Eagle, had eleven stores, ten thousand employees, and total sales of more than 3 billion yuan—or about $350 million. Golden Eagle sold stock on the Hong Kong Stock Exchange in 2006 to gain financing for growth and to set up a structure that will go on when Wang steps away. Now one of the richest men in China, Wang sums up his success by humbly recalling his schooling, formal and informal, in the United States and China: "The skills I acquired in Southeastern Louisiana University, Thrifty Drugs, and selling insurance along with knowing the history, behavior and local staff helped make Golden Eagle a success story."

For more than a decade, Wang has spent eight months of every year in China and only four months in California. He says that now he spends more time in Beverly Hills—but he is not retiring. On the contrary, he has started a fashion business that gives exposure in China to U.S. designers and clothiers like Vera Wang and Victoria's Secret and Sabrina Kay, the young Korean American entrepreneur we met in Chapter 3. "I can showcase the fashions inexpensively in my stores," says Wang, who has opened a showroom in Shanghai. So fashions designed in the United States and sewn partly in China and other countries tap into Chinese retail markets, which are growing 27 percent a year. It is a business that banker Ng sums up as a new force in the world: "That is not simply trade," he says. "It's an exchange of American business principles and ideas inspiring China."

Confucian Principles

If China has been inspired to change, so has the Chinese American community, which is engaged not only in business but in social and philanthropic activities in the broad American community. This is a departure from the past when Asian people kept to themselves out of choice and sad necessity. Ng, for example, is a member of a committee advising Governor Arnold Schwarzenegger on financial policy and throughout this decade has led and inspired United Way of Greater Los Angeles. The first Asian American to chair its campaign, Ng broadened its appeal to minority and entrepreneural individuals. Donald Tang is a trustee of Caltech, the Los Angeles County Museum of Art, and the RAND Corp.

Perhaps most significantly, Ng and Tang are members of the Committee of 100, an organization of American citizens of Chinese descent who since 1990—after the events of 1989 in Beijing's Tiananmen Square—have worked to increase knowledge and communications between the United States and China. The committee, with an eye to dismal nineteenth-century history, works to prevent prejudice. For example, the committee was successful in 1996 in countering false accusations of improper campaign contributions that were targeted at Chinese business-people. More than reacting to discrimination, the one hundred leading Chinese Americans—including the musician Yo-Yo Ma, architect I. M. Pei, former governor of Washington Gary Locke, and business leaders like Ng and Tang—seek to foster Americans' knowledge of Chinese culture.[16] In particular, the organization encourages schools to include Asian history in their curricula. A current enthusiasm for teaching the Chinese language in Los Angeles–area high schools is all to the good, Ng says, but the language itself is not the aim of his effort. "We would like simply to increase knowledge and appreciation of Asian cultures," he says, "and get away from the Eurocentric focus of the past."

Tang, who is in close touch with political and social thought in China, sees attitudes among entrepreneurial Chinese immigrants at first conflicting with the love of order and stability enshrined in the writings of K'ung Fu-tzu, the sage known in the West as Confucius. "Confucius theory is all about order, but American philosophy challenges order, says do what I can to win," Tang says. "When Chinese come here, they are entrepreneurs, not sanctioned by anybody as they might be by family if they were back in China. But the Confucian values stay with them because it is their ancestors, it is the culture. Confucian morality decrees that you respect your parents; education is king, family is all important. You may be very entrepreneurial, but to have moral authority, benevolence is extremely important." In the best of Chinese American businesses and organizations, Tang finds an emerging combination of American dynamism and Confucian benevolence.

Two remarkable Chinese immigrant–led companies in Southern California suggest this economic and social consciousness. The first is Panda Restaurant Group, one of the most interesting companies in the United States.[17] The Panda Express chain of quick-service restaurants, which now has more than 1,100 outlets, could not have happened in China—and it had never happened before in the United States. The business began, like many stories in this book, with young people coming to America. Andrew Cherng came from Taiwan in 1966 to attend Baker University, a small Methodist college in Baldwin City, Kansas, southwest of Kansas City. He is the son of Ming-tsai Cherng, a renowned chef who worked in the finest restaurants in Shanghai, Taipei, and Taiwan and then in Yokohama, Japan. But Andrew didn't think at the time of a future in restaurants. He came to study applied mathematics at Baker and later at the University of Missouri.

While at Baker, he met Peggy Tsiang, who had come to the school from Hong Kong. She studied mathematics and engineering at Baker and ultimately earned a master's degree in computer science and a doctorate in electrical engineering at the University of Missouri. Peggy and Andrew married shortly after graduation from Missouri and moved to Los Angeles where Peggy worked as a software developer for McDonnell Douglas and Andrew worked for his cousin, who owned a Chinese restaurant, while making plans for his father and mother to immigrate to the United States. After his father arrived, Andrew bought a shuttered coffee shop in Pasadena in 1973 and with his father turned it into a restaurant named Panda Inn. The menu, featuring Mandarin and Szechwan specialties, was different from the traditional Cantonese fare of most Chinese restaurants at the time.

"The hardest times are starting the business," Andrew Cherng says. He didn't want to lose any customers, he recalls. When customers turned away from Panda Inn because the tables were full, he went after them. "We had a back door to the restaurant, and I would go into the parking lot and say, 'Thank you for coming. I'm sorry we're crowded, but if you'll wait, I'll buy you a drink.' And they might return to the restaurant, saying, 'Wow, all this for our business!'" he says with a big smile, still surprised at his mastery of Marketing 101. Panda Inn flourished, and Cherng (shown in Figure 5.3) opened a second site in nearby Glendale in 1982 that attracted the real estate developers of Glendale Galleria, a shopping mall. They asked whether Panda's excellent cooking could be adapted to the fast-food court in their new mall. Ming-tsai Cherng had died two years before, but her son had learned by that time how to build a staff of chefs and Peggy had come in to manage the growing restaurant business. So together they took the challenge of bringing innovation to "Chinese take-out." And they succeeded. Where most attempts at Chinese fast food had settled for egg rolls, rice, and chow mein, the new venture, called Panda Express, offered orange-flavored chicken, tofu with black mushrooms, and many other dishes conceived and prepared on-site by cooks trained in Chinese cuisine. Panda Express was an instant attraction.

A quarter century later, the chain's success remains impressive, with 1,136 outlets, including twenty-seven Hibachi-san stores for Japanese meals, stretched over thirty-six states and Japan. Annual sales

Figure 5.3. Peggy and Andrew Cherng, founders and owners of Panda Express, at one of the chain's restaurants. Courtesy of the Panda Restaurant Group.

are more than $1 billion. It is already the largest food chain in history that is based on Chinese food. To be sure, with the growth of Chinese and Asian communities in the United States, it was inevitable that the market for quality Chinese foods would increase. Panda Express does not have the field entirely to itself, however. P. F. Chang's China Bistro restaurants, a company that serves American variations on Chinese dishes, and its Pei Wei Asian Diners chain, which serves fast food, have several hundred outlets in many parts of the country. But they haven't been able to match the growth and spread of Panda Express. Nor do they have the ambitions that the Cherngs, now in their early sixties, still have of building an American institution. "Chinese food is not on Americans' weekly to-do list yet, but it could be," Andrew says. "We can grow 20 percent a year," Peggy says, "to eventually ten thousand stores worldwide. We want to build a premier company with a good, distinct culture." The Panda firm now has almost twenty thousand employees, some part time. "Twenty percent of the shares are set aside for employees' ownership," Peggy adds. Remarkably, she is speaking of what is still a family-owned company. Aside from the Panda outlets in Japan, and a few licensed stores, the Cherngs still own all of the other restaurants. The company has expanded constantly out of its own cash flow. It has not sold stock to the public nor taken on major outside financing. "We would only sell stock if we needed capital, but we don't," says Peggy, who has led the corporate development of the group. In 2004, Andrew and Peggy appointed a professional chief executive, Tom Davin, a veteran of Pepsico and Taco Bell as well as financial businesses, to manage their growing company.

These days, with the titles of chairman for Andrew and cochair for Peggy, they devote some part of their energies and time to Panda Cares, a charitable effort dedicated to meeting the health and education needs of underserved children. In addition, the organization mobilizes volunteers and relief efforts to help during worldwide natural disasters, such as the 2008 earthquake in China and cyclone in Myanmar as well as Hurricane Katrina and the 2004 tsunami in the Indian Ocean.

Panda Cares resembles programs at McDonald's, another American institution that originated in Southern California. "We're not at McDonald's level yet," Peggy says, "but yes, we hire people and pay benefits and make sure we become part of the community. And we provide career paths within the company." A successful Panda general manager "can earn $100,000 in profit sharing," she says. But the Cherngs' programs for hiring and training employees are much more than routine human resources efforts. "We ask our employees not only how you're working, but how are you living?" Andrew says. "How do you improve mentally, physically, emotionally, spiritually? The biggest thing we are focused on is personal growth. How do we help people become better human beings? If you become a better human being, you are able to do your job better. This approach is new to us, but it is very clear today that we need to do this."

The Cherngs' thinking about policies toward employees and their company stems from the books of Stephen R. Covey, a motivational author and business consultant. The Cherngs give copies of his book *The 7 Habits of Highly Effective People* to visitors at Panda headquarters in Rosemead, California. The central message of Covey's books is that the virtues that count in business are those that count in life: "integrity, humility, fidelity, temperance, courage, justice, simplicity and patience." These surely are attitudes that most employers would look for in prospective workers. But perhaps just because they are Chinese and new to America, it is impossible not to hear in the Cherngs thoughts about employees and the company echoes of Confucius, who lived and spoke twenty-four hundred years ago. "Sincerity is the beginning and end of all things," it says in the *Doctrine of the Mean*, or *The Golden Mean*, one of the main books of the Confucian canon.[18] To achieve virtue, Confucius counseled people to "practice five things: gravity, generosity of soul, sincerity, earnestness and kindness." Indeed, such sentiments run like a thread through the ambitions not only of the Cherngs but of Donald Tang and Dominic Ng and of the late Henry Hwang, who translated the U.S. Constitution for customers and shareholders of his bank.

Needs of the Community

The same sentiments are evident in the thinking of John Long, founder of Highridge Partners, a real estate investment firm in Los Angeles and other ventures. Long came to the United States as a boy of seven in 1954 when, as he noted in 2006, "Chinese people could not own property."

The law prohibiting Chinese from owning property had been declared unconstitutional by the U.S. Supreme Court in 1948, but the California legislature would not repeal the unjust law until 1956, two years after Long arrived from Canton (now Guangzhou). Because of this and other discriminatory practices, his father and uncles, though successful grocery store merchants in the United States at the time, had no avenue for investing their profits in America. As a result, Long's family took their U.S. savings and invested in real estate in Canton. Mao Tse-tung's Communist government, which came to power in 1949, took away the family's real estate holdings and forced Long to move to the United States. Because the family fortune was confiscated, Long grew up in an inner-city neighborhood in South Los Angeles. But he was bright and determined and went on to study economics at UCLA and then to earn an MBA from Harvard Business School. "I didn't know what I really wanted to do, but coming from my background, I wanted to be in business of some sort," Long says.[19]

The business he chose was real estate. In 1971, he went to work for Kaufman & Broad, a homebuilder (now KB Home Inc.), and in 1978 he formed Highridge Partners. Long and five associates began investing in commercial real estate. "We wanted to be owners. We would identify assets, negotiate a purchase, lease it out, develop it, from soup to nuts, and sell it," Long recalls in his small, bright office in a Los Angeles–area industrial park that he helped create. Property ownership has been profitable. Over twenty-eight years, Long and his partners amassed more than $6 billion worth of real estate in California, and later in Texas in the early 1990s when California real estate faltered. They have bought and sold shrewdly and multiplied their investments more than one thousand times.

In 2005, Long then turned to what he sees as a growth market for real estate: Southern California's expanding Latino communities. Highridge Partners created a joint venture with boxer Oscar De La Hoya's business enterprises to form Golden Boy Partners. Together, the investor and the boxer have invested $100 million over three years to build in Latino neighborhoods. "Today's Latino neighborhoods don't reflect the vibrancy and energy of their residents," Long says. "We are going to rebuild and build new in such neighborhoods to revitalize them with affordable homes and commercial businesses." The ambition of the Chinese and Latino formerly poor kids is broad and idealistic. "In this investment we are creating a vision for Latino society, a philosophy of investment for Latino society," says Long.

That social impulse is a theme for the two institutes on which Long has focused his philanthropic energies at his alma mater, UCLA. The first is the Ziman Center for Real Estate that Long founded in 2000 and today remains its founding chairman. For "this $20 trillion industry," as he calls real estate, Long established a multidisciplinary center unique among universities. Unlike most real estate institutes, the center won't study property prices or deal making or even architecture per se, but how people live. "The choice of the next generation will be urban," Long says. "Business is a driver of social change. And today, technology and capital flows empower entrepreneurs as never before. We need to study real estate in relation to finance, the environment and the legal system and technology—the Internet—and to the choices people will have to make."

The second research center Long is creating at UCLA is the US-China Institute for Business and Policy. "We are just starting to explore opportunities in China," Long says. "It is another fascinating journey." His idea of the US-China Institute, Long said in an overview presented to university administrators in China and at UCLA, is that it will be a place where Chinese and American scholars, businesspeople, and public officials can "gain understanding of the policies and challenges that engage them in business and government, legal and technological developments." The institute will support academic research among all the University of California campuses and at universities in China. It will work with students in both countries to create, as Long and Archie Kleingartner of UCLA's Anderson School of Management put it, "a more positive binational economic platform." In other words, the US-China Institute is one more development in the growing collaboration of Southern California and the United States with China and Asia, which is political, social, and philosophical as much as it is economical.

Significantly, Long, an immigrant to the States, has seen the university as the center for advancing knowledge of business and industry and national and international purposes. For it is the country's universities during the half century since World War II that have become centers of basic research for advancing technology and knowledge in all areas of the economy and society. The next chapter relates how the many centers of higher learning in Southern California have expanded the role of the university in the transformation of the world economy.

6 Universities
Engines of the New Economy

> Access to the newest and best knowledge is the secret to
> global success for many industries and is best obtained inside
> the universities where there is the new knowledge and the
> people who create, share, and learn it.
>
> Clark Kerr,
chancellor, University of California, Berkeley,
and president, University of California system

SOUTHERN CALIFORNIA'S universities are key players
furthering America's connections to Asia and Latin
America. For more than a decade, the University of Southern California;
the University of California, Los Angeles; and the University of California, Irvine, have had programs in which their professors teach classes at
universities in China. All have run joint research programs with scholars
in Asia and have welcomed large numbers of students from Asia.

Now these universities are taking collaboration a step further by
developing a practical vision of global teaching. They are demonstrating how teaching industrial systems, finance, and engineering across
national boundaries promises to be one of America's greatest exports
for the new world economy. In a breakthrough program, the UCLA
Anderson School of Management and the National University of Singapore (NUS) provide the opportunity for executive MBA students from
many countries to take classes in Singapore and Los Angeles, and also
in Shanghai and Bangalore, India. "We're creating a business school

in a global context," Judy Olian, dean of the Anderson School, told me. "We want to create effective leadership for global organizations—businesses or governmental and nongovernmental organizations. That has not been thought of as the mission of business schools, but it is in the emerging world of today."[1]

USC now awards a Global MBA in Shanghai, where executive candidates from ten countries attend classes taught by USC professors. The students also come to Los Angeles for part of the intensive, twenty-month program, which has been running since 2004. Schools and governments of other countries have approached USC to organize similar programs for them. C. L. Max Nikias, provost and senior vice president for academic affairs of USC, says that he sees the global initiatives as a natural extension of the university's mission for this time and place: "Our strategic plan calls for us to capitalize more fully on our location at a global crossroads and on our uniquely international heritage, so that USC can emerge as a truly global university: one with students prepared for world citizenship; one with faculty members who can cross academic and geographic boundaries in order to innovate; one with a public-service mission that spans continents."[2]

The Paul Merage School of Business at the University of California, Irvine (UCI), which has been sending its students on residency programs abroad for two decades, now devises class work designed to give its eight hundred MBA candidates—35 percent of whom are not U.S. residents—a mindset that is "global" as opposed to "foreign." An example is the "egg drop test." "In our global access courses," Dean Andrew Policano told me, "we challenge teams, in a language that is not that of the United States, to drop an egg from two stories without breaking it. One must learn to innovate with other cultures." Policano feels that "the biggest difficulties in international business ventures are not technology or even economic systems but diversity of culture." The Merage School holds collaborative ventures with universities in the United States and overseas and organizes conferences in India and China. "In China a new foreign-owned factory opens every twenty-six minutes; every forty-three hours in China, a new research and development lab opens. How do businesses not only survive but thrive in this global innovation economy?" asks Policano, an economist and mathematician who helped the school's founder, Paul Merage, devise the school's approach to teaching business.[3]

This chapter describes and affirms the role of Southern California's universities as foundations of the economy in this region, in the country, and in the world. During the decades after World War II, these universities became centers of every kind of scientific and technological development, including space exploration, orbital satellite communication, the discovery of the Internet, and the genetic engineering of human cells. The globalization of teaching is but the latest extension of the universities' roles in research and commercialization.

Clark Kerr, a leader of the University of California system, defined new roles for academe in 1963 in his book *The Uses of the University*. Kerr saw what he called the "multiversity" as a new kind of institution that was really neither private nor public but endowed with a mission to do research work for the progress of science and society—as well as to educate students. Kerr, who was an economist, saw collaborations of institutions like Caltech and UC Berkeley with Pentagon and NASA projects as emblematic. During World War I, Kerr noted, "the universities had only been a source of raw recruits." But during World War II, with national laboratories established at campuses in Massachusetts, Illinois, and California, "the major universities were enlisted in national defense and in scientific and technological development as never before." The universities were not discharged from service when the war ended. In the 1950s, Kerr observed an increase of government grants to schools of the University of California system to fund medical and sociological research as well as defense programs. And he saw the beginnings of the trend that has flourished nationally as corporations began financing basic research at universities and the schools set up agencies to commercialize the results of faculty and student projects. Increasingly today, large philanthropic donations add to the flow of capital that undergirds the research university model.[4]

Knowledge as Capital

Southern California has more research universities than any location in the United States, with five members of the University of California system and independent universities like USC, Caltech, and the Claremont Colleges and Graduate University, to name a few. Southern California did not "invent" the knowledge economy, but a noted professor here coined the term. Peter F. Drucker, the management scholar who taught at Claremont Graduate University for thirty-four years until his death in 2005, saw as early as 1960 that the "basic economic resource of the new economy . . . is and will be knowledge" and not the classic triumvirate of land, labor, and capital.[5] He was referring to the primacy of software, design, and communications in contemporary industries. Just as the old Industrial Revolution needed factories, so the knowledge economy needs colleges and universities.

Today, these colleges and universities are determinedly international. Southern California is a leader in the nationwide enrollment of more than 550,000 foreign students at U.S. universities. USC leads the country in international students, with 20 percent of its total enrollment, at undergraduate and graduate levels, coming from countries around the world. More than 10 percent of UCLA's student body comes from abroad.[6] These numbers are on the rise again after a drop-off following 9/11, when restrictions tightened on student visas for entering the United States. "A degree from an American university, from U.C.L.A., is highly valued in Asia," says Ronson Wong, an executive of Reach Global Services, a Hong Kong–based provider of cable and satellite communications in Asia. Wong recently completed studies for the dual MBA degrees from UCLA and NUS. He is expressing a view of U.S. education that is just about universal among international businesspeople. Why are American universities so highly prized abroad? "We have a different kind of pedagogy," says James Ellis, dean of USC's Marshall School of Business. "We are much more inclusive of students, allowing their participation on many levels, in contrast to the classic Oxford lecture model. The students learn from one another, particularly in the global classes where individuals from different cultures work together."[7]

One of the most interesting examples of students operating on a worldwide scale is the Global Access Program (GAP) at UCLA's Anderson School. The program enrolls 175 MBA candidates who are fully employed during the three years it takes them to earn their degrees, doing coursework fifteen to eighteen hours a week in addition to their full-time jobs. Their average age is about thirty-three, and the "global access" in the program's title is far more than the traditional semester abroad of college students. GAP students consult for six months at a time for international companies that want to get into the U.S. market or simply "operate beyond their current borders," explains Robert Foster, dean of the fully employed MBA program (FEMBA).[8] The students, who work in teams of five or six, average five hundred hours of work on a typical project. In its first decade, the program completed 207 projects. As an example of a FEMBA project, Formthotics, Inc., a New Zealand company, had an orthopedic shoe insole that it believed would be a good addition to the athletic footwear market in the United States. For a contribution of $12,500 to cover expenses, it hired a FEMBA team to gauge its chances in the U.S. market. The UCLA team found that there wasn't really much opportunity to bring another athletic product to a crowded U.S. market. But the students contacted the American Diabetes Foundation, which determined that the sensitivity of Formthotics insoles to heat and pressure could offer early warnings to incipient diabetes patients and help them avoid later amputations, said Elwin Svenson, a retired UCLA provost who is working with GAP. In another GAP project, students studied markets in Russia for the Technology Agency of finland, a government office, on behalf of software, communications, and construction services firms. Why would finland hire American students to study a market in Russia? Because the Americans "know how to commercialize technology, to map out the complex of distribution channels, marketing, and finance that any product needs to be successful," says Foster, who was chief executive of a Los Angeles company before moving into academic life at UCLA. GAP is expanding in 2008 to 240 students and forty-eight company projects, reaching out to India and China, Mexico, Spain, and Austria for new companies and opportunities.

Technology Transfer

Over recent decades, Southern California's universities have become adept at turning technologies into businesses, a process called *technology transfer* that was officially authorized by Congress in the Bayh-Dole Act of 1980. That law granted universities the right to own, license, and market the fruits of their faculty research, even if that research was financed by the Defense Department or another arm of the federal government. (Figure 6.1 shows amounts of government grants to universities to spur technological development.) Bayh-Dole created possibilities, and the marketplace did the rest, as university researchers soon came in contact with investors of venture capital. (Figure 6.2 shows the increase in the number of patent applications filed by universities working with government and industry research funds.) A most interesting example

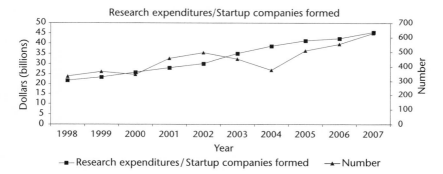

Figure 6.1. Research grants, mainly from government, to universities in order to spur technological development and the number of startup companies formed as a result of technology transfer. Source: Author's calculations based on the Association of University Technology Managers, Licensing Surveys.

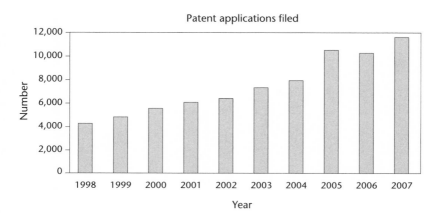

Figure 6.2. Growth of the number of patent applications filed by universities working with government and industry research funds. Source: Author's calculations based on the Association of University Technology Managers, Licensing Surveys.

of the technology transfer process starts with Arnold Orville Beckman, who pioneered the idea of the university as a source of economic progress long before it became obvious during the post–World War II era. In 1935, while an assistant professor of chemistry at Caltech, Beckman invented an electronic pH meter to measure the acidity of lemon juice for a friend who worked with the California Fruit Growers Exchange. Acidity levels were important to the growers, who needed a reliable method of measuring the taste of the fruit. Beckman's invention gave the state's agriculture industry a reliable measurement tool and directly and indirectly gave California decades of industrial leadership.

Beckman and Caltech's efforts on behalf of the citrus industry were anticipated by the Citrus Experiment Station, set up at Riverside, California, in 1907 by the state government to help the growers of the area's navel oranges. The citrus station's research evolved into a center of graduate study, then a College of Letters and Sciences, and ultimately, in 1959, to the University of California, Riverside (UCR). Today, UCR has seventeen thousand students, and its research efforts have contributed forty varieties of citrus to California's bounty.

Beckman, however, was as much businessman as academic scientist. He saw that his photoelectric meter had broad applications beyond lemons because it gave scientists the ability to measure all kinds of ingredients in experiments. He decided to sell his meters for $195 apiece through a private business venture, which defied expectations and made a profit in 1936 by selling 444 meters. That venture became the foundation of Beckman Instruments, a company that made numerous breakthroughs in scientific and medical instruments and provided the foundation for other companies such as Shockley Semiconductor, an originator of Silicon Valley, and General Instruments, a key innovator of electronics for cable and satellite television. Beckman, who lived to age 104, went on to make enormous contributions to Caltech and other universities and to encourage students to develop businesses from their research work.[9]

Caltech itself became a leading practitioner of Beckman's ideas. Founded in 1891 as the Throop College of Technology, the Pasadena school became Caltech in 1921 as grants from the Rockefeller and Carnegie foundations supported its research. It rose to national stature during World War II as a laboratory for inventing advanced weaponry, particularly rockets. In postwar America, Caltech epitomized the new model of private school–public purpose. In the late 1940s, for example, Arie J. Haagen-Smit, a Caltech biochemist, identified the smog that was withering foliage along Los Angeles highways and set the ball rolling toward programs to reduce air pollution. Over many decades, Caltech faculty members have been responsible for more than one hundred patents each year; the institute holds almost two thousand patents at present.

Yet it was not until the 1990s, after Defense Department and other government grants diminished, that the school organized its Office of Technology Transfer to foster commercial development of Caltech discoveries. The effort has produced impressive results, with Caltech spawning eighty new companies in the past decade. They include Calando Pharmaceuticals, which commercialized a cancer treatment developed by Mark Davis of Caltech, the founding scientist of Calando. The treatment involves ribonucleic acid in targeting and then "silencing" cancerous genes. The tech transfer program also backed another Davis company, Insert Therapeutics, which uses nanotechnology molecular structures to deliver drugs quickly and more safely to the source of illness.

Caltech is willing to help finance a startup company by taking shares itself. A recent example is Impinj Inc., which makes critical semiconductor-antenna chips that power radio frequency identification, or RfiD, tags. Such microscopic tags make it possible to continuously track products that enter U.S. ports or sit on the shelves of stores or in medical vials in hospitals. Seattle-based Impinj originated in research done at Caltech by Carver Mead, one of the founders of modern electronics, and a student of his, Christopher Diorio, who is now professor of computer science at the University of Washington and chairman of Impinj. To start the company in 2001, "Caltech took a small equity stake," says William Colleran, president and chief executive of Impinj. The university was not investing in specific technology but in potential. "Initially, we were working with a communications chip," Colleran explains, "but in 2003 when the government began to mandate RfiD, we saw that our technology could be the perfect product." Impinj has 150 employees and an annual revenue of about $30 million. It also has $75 million in venture capital from nine major funds and hopes one day to sell stock publicly, which "would provide a return for all those investors, including Caltech," Colleran points out.

The equity investment by Caltech was in lieu of fees for acquiring a patent—usually about $20,000. Caltech also defers license fees until a company gets on its feet. "Our aim is to help the entrepreneurs get started; they need to retain all the cash they can," says Frederic Farina, who is now assistant vice president of Caltech and director of the technology transfer office. The economic payoff for the university in the short term lies in "fees and royalties from licensing patents," says Lawrence H. Gilbert, the first director of Caltech's transfer office, who has now retired. But "the real benefit," he adds, "comes from contributions to the endowment if the startup company is successful."[10]

Another example of technology transfer occurred in 1985 at UCSD, which set up an independent program called Connect that brought its professors together with the business and finance communities to examine interesting research being done at UCSD's medical and engineering schools. As a result, entrepreneurial companies in biotechnology were started, including Idec Pharmaceuticals—which today, as Biogen Idec, has become a major developer of drugs and treatments for cancer and autoimmune inflammatory diseases. Amylin Pharmaceuticals, developer of a substitute for insulin, was started with a helping hand from Connect. And so were more than eight hundred companies to date in a twenty-two-year history of the Connect program, which has become a model for other universities in California and worldwide.[11]

Connect with Ventures
Note well, the Connect program does not provide financing for startup companies. The venture capital firms and banks that come to its meetings with UCSD researchers do the financing. Connect also does not specify research areas for the university nor function as a commission-earning go-between for financial backers of new companies; Connect is not an agent. Connect also is not financed by the university, either through the state-funded portion of its income or its private donor endowment. Instead, Connect finances itself through contributions from the companies and venture capital funds that value the connections to university research. The investment companies involved with Connect,

like the startups they back, are relatively small venture capital funds and banking firms. They are angel groups that invest seed money in entrepreneurial ventures. Above all, the San Diego area—where the big university and several smaller schools are cheek by jowl with scientific foundations like the Scripps Research Institute, the Salk Institute for Biological Studies, and the Burnham Institute for Medical Research— provides a community of intellectual and scientific inquiry where ideas may contend and flourish. The late Bill Otterson, a computer entrepreneur who developed the Connect program over thirteen years during the 1980s and 1990s, was always modest about the program's achievements. "Would entrepreneurs have founded companies without Connect? I'm sure they would," he used to say.

An environment that fosters inquiry "is essential," says Stanford University economic philosopher Paul Romer. "The Chinese had movable type four hundred years before Gutenberg," Romer notes. "Nevertheless, the political and social system in China at that time provided no incentives for additional discovery."[12] But in Europe, the invention of movable type and printing spurred the expansion of knowledge. Political and social systems changed profoundly because more individuals than ever had access to manuscripts and books. Indeed, the playwright George Bernard Shaw in *St. Joan* credited the invention of printing with the Protestant Reformation, the rise of the nation-state, and the spread of democracy. One need not entertain such vaulting intellectual connections to understand that societies which reward innovation get what they pay for.

A company formed in 2003 by three UCSD researchers illustrates how a university environment can contribute to the invention of new technology. Tinnitus Otosound Products began in the research of Erik Viirre, a medical doctor who found that tinnitus, or ringing in the ears, occurs not in the ears at all, but in the brain. To combat the affliction, which is an often-debilitating ailment for more than 30 million Americans, Viirre consulted with two university colleagues, Jaime A. Pineda and F. Richard Moore, who were pursuing other research on auditory problems. They theorized that generating external sound in a machine to exactly match the frequency of the sound in the patient's brain could cause the original ringing to diminish or cease. They tested treatments on volunteer patients and came up with Customized Sound Therapy, which is able to mitigate tinnitus. The university acquired a patent in their names and that of the university, and the company has operated thus far on about $550,000 in grants, refining its technology and conducting trials for the Food and Drug Administration so that the therapy can be classed as a medical treatment as opposed to only a mitigation device. If Tinnitus Otosound succeeds, UCSD will receive a royalty of 5 percent of the company's revenue, which will go toward financing more research.[13]

USC in two of its research institutes provides yet another example of technology transfer. Its Information Sciences Institute (ISI), which the university inherited thirty-three years ago from the RAND Corp., works on basic and applied research in projects funded by government and industry. Among other breakthroughs, ISI played a dominant role in the creation of the domain name system of computing networking—the familiar ".com," ".net," and ".edu" designations in e-mail and Web addresses. ISI is a key recipient of the $440 million a year in research grants that USC receives from government and industry.

Neven Vision, which was developed partly at ISI, is an outstanding example of the fecund potential of research shared by universities in the United States and Europe plus U.S. government grants and private capital markets working together. The company was created by Hartmut Neven, a physicist who worked on the science of facial recognition—biometric analysis of facial features, skin tones, and the eye's iris—to make possible machine-vision representations of people and objects. He was brought to USC through a collaboration with the University of Bochum in Germany and worked on his technology at ISI with support from the Pentagon. As his development of machine-vision identification for military and homeland security purposes succeeded, Neven adapted the technologies to lower-cost versions that could be transmitted on cellular telephones. Ultimately, Neven says, the technology "will allow you to point your camera phone at a movie poster or a restaurant and get an immediate review of the film or the fare on your cellphone, which will tap into databases." He foresees 1 billion camera phones in use worldwide by 2010. Neven organized a company in 2004 to commercialize facial recognition technology that was financed with venture capital from Anthem Venture

Partners and Zone Ventures, two funds based a few miles from ISI. In August 2006, Neven Vision was acquired for more than $40 million by Google Inc., which saw possibilities in Neven's vision for receiving images in response to a search request instead of data.

Technology transfer has clearly paid off for Neven and his company's financial backers. But what do the universities get out of it? The benefits to USC include potential licensing fees from patents on the developing technology and the possibility of contributions to the university from successful entrepreneurs like Neven. "With more than $400 million a year in research at this university, we should be creating more commercial applications and spin-off revenues," Provost Max Nikias told me. Accordingly, Nikias in 2006 reached out to recruit Krisztina "Z" Holly, a mechanical engineer and entrepreneur and founder of the Deshpande Center for Technological Innovation at the Massachusetts Institute of Technology, where she developed a method of recognizing and adapting innovative technology from research to commercial ventures. At USC Holly heads the Stevens Institute for Innovation, a university-wide resource designed to translate ideas from USC into something that tangibly affects society. USC Stevens was founded in 2006 with a $22 million gift from Mark Stevens, a USC graduate and venture capitalist who has backed twenty-two companies in a variety of fields. Transferring university research into startup companies and nonprofits is a way to "convey to the public benefits of research that in many cases has been developed with public money," Holly says. She cites research showing that companies organized in collaboration between universities and the financial world generated $34 billion in economic value and almost three hundred thousand jobs over the 1980s and 1990s. The USC Stevens Institute "encourages entrepreneurship in all the schools of the university, the social sciences and media and law as well," she says.[14]

A case in point is the work of Roberta Diaz Brinton, a Ph.D. in psychobiology and neuropharmacology who has labored for more than a quarter century to find ways to combat memory loss and ultimately Alzheimer's disease, particularly among women, who account for 68 percent of the 18 million sufferers of Alzheimer's worldwide. Obviously, it is not a simple problem. Brinton and her staff at the neuroscience laboratory at USC know that estrogen therapy for postmenopausal women is a key to keeping brain cells active and lively. But such hormone replacement therapy might contribute to breast and uterine cancers. So they have been working to find a safe estrogen replacement. Brinton explains that her lab is closest to achieving a safe therapeutic strategy by using molecules occurring in nature, which she terms phytoSERMs (*phyto* for plant-derived and *SERMs* for selective estrogen receptor modulators), and by generating novel formulations of these molecules to promote the benefit of estrogen in the brain without adverse effects in the breasts or uterus. She and her team are also designing novel estrogens for the brain, called neuroSERMS, and have discovered a molecule, called neurogen, that will promote the generation of new neurons and regenerate memory circuits in the brains of men as well as women. Another conclusion of her research is that the time to give such estrogen replacement therapy to women is during middle age, before menopause rather than after. That way, cells are kept healthy and resistant to the "degenerative insults to brain cells" that come with aging, Brinton says.

Long-Term Backing

Brinton's intense scientific work is funded by the National Institutes of Health and the Alzheimer's Drug Discovery Foundation. But new funding is needed to take her promising therapies through clinical trials for the Food and Drug Administration, which could cost $1.5 million for each therapy. That's why she is talking to venture capital financiers with the support of the USC Stevens Institute. Paying for clinical trials is not something venture capital firms, which must earn a high return, do very often. But times are changing, Holly says, and "today it is possible if difficult to find the right investors for sophisticated, long-term research like this. There are benefits to raising philanthropic gifts to support early-stage ideas through the proof-of-concept stage, especially in the life sciences," Holly adds. "USC is planning a transitional fund patterned after the Deshpande Center for this very reason." An energetic newcomer to technology transfer is the graduate school of management at UCI, which changed its focus, and its name, at the urging of entrepreneur and philanthropist Paul Merage. An immigrant from Iran, Merage invented the microwaveable snack meal Hot Pockets while working as an executive in the food-processing industry. He donated

$30 million to UCI in 2005 with a stipulation that the business school, now the Paul Merage School of Business, add a stress on innovation and "ways to grow a business" to its traditional curriculum of accounting, finance, and marketing.[15]

In a relatively short time, the Merage School has developed an entrepreneurship center that produces dozens of new companies a year, particularly in the burgeoning field of health care. One such company is OCT Medical Imaging, which is able, through a technology called optical coherence tomography (OCT), to record detailed images of tissues near the surface of the body. OCT uses a powerful light beam that shines 2 to 3 millimeters into most body tissues. Computer analysis of the reflected light creates images that are detailed enough to reveal tiny cancers or tissue structures that occur near the surface of the skin, eye, gastrointestinal tract, or larynx. The light is carried on fiber-optic probes small enough to be inserted through surgical devices into the lungs, veins, and arteries without requiring a hospital stay. "It is similar to ultrasound because it detects the echo of the wave coming back from different depths of tissue," Professor Zhongping Chen explains. "The difference is that ultrasound uses sound waves and OCT uses light waves." The company also has developed fiber-optic probes that fit inside biopsy needles, which could be used to look for tiny lung cancer cells during laparoscopic surgery. That could make immediate optical biopsies possible, as replacements for biopsies studied in laboratories after surgery.

Chen, born in Shanghai, is the vice chairman of UCI's biomedical engineering department and a physicist with ten patents for biomedical sensors. He formed OCT Medical Imaging with Ram Ramalingam, an immigrant from India who studied at the Indian Institute of Science and earned an MBA from the Merage School. They also partnered with Nathaniel Weiner, a dentist in Lakewood, California, and an entrepreneurial investor. UCI's Office of Technology Alliances was instrumental in starting the company. Of course, UCI, as part of the University of California system, imposes some rules aimed at avoiding conflict of interest for researchers whose inventions head to market. For example, faculty members like Chen can be cofounders of a company, but they cannot serve as one of the company's executives or on its board of directors.

In OCT's case, UCI required a $100,000 investment from Weiner before OCT Medical could license Chen's technology. But UCI contributed access to its world-class laboratories in helping the company get started and owns a small equity stake in OCT Medical. "Without the university, we would have nothing," Ramalingam says.

The universal drive to reduce the costs of health care, now a giant segment of the U.S. economy worth $2 trillion a year, has inspired several companies started by entrepreneurial students at Merage. One is Manette Quinn, a 2006 MBA graduate who founded MediQuin Credentialing Services. The company provides verification of health records for hospitals and health maintenance organizations, thus saving time and money. Another is Maya Gowri, a successful businesswoman in India who came to the United States to earn a doctorate in biology from the University of Kentucky and an MBA from Merage. The MBA studies "taught me about function and marketing and helped me find a business partner to raise finance," Gowri says. In 2006, she founded Discovery Services International, a firm that performs research for small biotechnology companies, with fund-raising help from Charles Hsu, a venture capitalist who was at Merage to earn his MBA.

Quinn's and Gowri's companies make use of the Internet to develop innovations for the health-care field. "The possibilities of the Net are as broad as all industry," observes Ian Chaplin, who is a graduate of UCSD with degrees in biology and genetic engineering and an entrepreneur who has started sixteen companies in the past decade. They include BidShift, a hiring exchange for hospitals and nurses. BidShift provides a solution to a problem hospitals have with rigid and expensive hourly pay rates for nurses whom they need on short notice. Nurses also frequently prefer to work irregular schedules. The BidShift Website allows hospitals and nurses to negotiate acceptable hourly rates and schedules. Thus, the Internet serves as labor union, management, and business consultant all in one.[16]

Sources of Employment

Society's economic payoff from all the university efforts focused on technology and entrepreneurship is impressive. In California, high-technology categories in the information and biological sciences now account for more than 3 million jobs, more than 20 percent of the state's total. And high-tech categories are the fastest-growing sources of employment—rising almost 60 percent in the past decade in San Diego County, more than 50 percent in Orange County, and by more than 120,000 jobs or nearly 25 percent in highly developed Los Angeles County. Moreover, the broader self-definition of the university is paying off handsomely for the state's institutions of higher learning, according to a 2006 study by the Santa Monica–based Milken Institute. The study, which covered the years 2000 to 2004, measured patents issued to university discoveries, licenses granted and income from licenses to the schools, and the number of startup companies launched by individual universities. The University of California system—all nine campuses—and Caltech rank higher than any other institutions in patents issued, although the Massachusetts Institute of Technology had a higher aggregate score based on all the categories. Stanford University ranked fourth, as California schools led the worldwide list, with six places among the top twenty-five universities.[17]

The state of California has been exemplary in supporting university research projects over extended periods and in following through to keep up with technological evolution. In 2000, the state launched a plan to spur university research programs that shared the costs with federal grants and donations from private industry and philanthropic foundations. To begin with, California gave $100 million to each of four Governor Gray Davis Institutes for Science and Innovation, which include the California NanoSystems Institute, located at UCLA and UC Santa Barbara; the California Institute for Telecommunications and Information Technology, at UCI and UCSD; the California Institute for Quantitative Biosciences at UC San Francisco, Berkeley, and Santa Cruz; and the Center for Information Technology Research in the Interest of Society at UC Davis, Merced, Berkeley, and Santa Cruz. The efforts were also backed by $110 million to each group from the federal government and about $50 million from private corporations, including Hewlett-Packard, Intel, Amgen, and Ericsson of Sweden. "The idea is that the next generations of new enterprises that are science and technology based will come out of collaborations of the great research universities and government and the private sector," Albert Carnesale, UCLA's chancellor at the time, said in 2001.[18]

And so they have. The initial nanotechnology effort has been followed by larger programs, including one in which UC Berkeley and Stanford joined UCLA and UC Santa Barbara to establish the Western Institute of Nanoelectronics. The institute is working to produce semiconductors that move beyond the present transistor-loaded microchips to processes that move electrical charges in constant spinning motion. The prefix *nano* denotes one-billionth part; a nanometer, for example, is one-billionth of a meter. Nanotechnology refers to broad capabilities developed in the past decade to work at molecular levels in creating new approaches to practically every field. In manufacturing, nanoparticles are capable of forming machines that make products and processes—and other machines. In medicine, nanosystems are capable of working at the level of human cells, heralding a potential "fusion of nanotechnology and biology," writes UCLA professor Chih-Ming Ho in *Nanotechnology: Science, Innovation, and Opportunity,* a book that outlines the current state of the technology.[19] Ho heads UCLA's Center for Micro Systems, which has pioneered research in microelectromechanical systems and which is recognized as one of the best such centers in the world. In 2004, NASA chose UCLA as one of four centers for a ten-year program devoted to research in a variety of nanotechnology areas. The other three are Texas A&M, Princeton, and Purdue.

California also has a $3 billion voter-authorized program to back research in stem cells, which is spawning companies and laboratory efforts. One such company is International Stem Cell Corp., of Oceanside, California. Its chief scientist, Elena Revazova, developed a method of producing stem cells through chemical treatment of spare female eggs gathered in the process of in vitro fertilization. Revazova worked for almost forty years at leading biomedical institutes in Moscow. She left Russia in 1997 because the post-Soviet governments did not fund scientific research as the Communist regime of the Soviet Union always had. She moved to Los Angeles and found minor work at the UCLA Medical Center. But fellow researchers there soon discovered her talents and achievements and put her together with other scientists, as well as venture investors and business experts. The company they formed, with $11 million initially, is currently working with stem cells to mimic the insulin-producing processes of the pancreas as well as retinal cells for the inner eye and cells for the liver.[20] The company also is collaborating with Dr. Hans Kierstead at the Reeve-Irvine Research Center at UCI in his work to develop nerve cells. The institute is named for the late Christopher Reeve, the movie actor who was paralyzed after a fall from a horse and subsequently funded research in spinal cord injury and other neurological disorders. The full effects of California's $3 billion program and stem cell research are yet to be seen.

Business as Technology

University efforts are not restricted to the sciences. The relation between business disciplines and advanced technology is being recognized as an academic discipline as well. In 1997, the Keck Graduate Institute of Applied Life Sciences opened as the newest addition to the Claremont Colleges group. Its curriculum integrates business management with scientific courses to produce not more scientists but managers for the work that scientists do in biotechnology companies and other technical areas. The idea was reflected in 2001 at the opening of the Rady School of Management at UCSD. Its mission is to train managers for technology-based companies. "We want young people with a scientific and engineering bent," says Robert Sullivan, the dean. Also, it takes only one year to earn an MBA at Rady, compared with two at most other institutions. Sullivan notes that Wall Street powerhouses Goldman Sachs and Charles Schwab said "make your course shorter." Mary Walshok, overseer of UCSD's extension programs and a pioneer of the Connect program, adds, "A twenty-first-century business school should be focused on global technology and entrepreneurship." Appropriately, Pohang Steel Co. of South Korea set up a $250 million fund in 2001 to support not only biotechnology research at UCSD and other universities but the founding of entrepreneurial companies based on biotech innovation.[21]

Some of these new university programs have the philosophy that isolating science from art and practical public questions from intellectual pursuits is passé in the new industrial age. "At the university we must become transdisciplinary," says Robert Klitgaard, president of Claremont Graduate University (CGU). Klitgaard, an expert on economic development who has taught at Yale and Harvard, sees the role of the relatively small CGU—with its two thousand students—as "going across boundaries" to engage in research on public questions such as education, transportation, and health care. He explains that the economy, which through different ages has been based on agriculture, industry, and more recently, information, has now become a collaborative endeavor with numerous contributors. "Peter Drucker was transdisciplinary," Klitgaard says, referring to the visionary scholar who founded the Peter F. Drucker and Masatoshi Ito Graduate School of Management, which is part of CGU. In Drucker's name, CGU set up an institute to bring participants from all over the world together to make progress on global social and economic questions, particularly as such questions apply to San Bernardino and Riverside counties, the expanding Inland Empire region east of Los Angeles. The Drucker School's mission is another form of technology transfer, in keeping with the broader purposes of the university in this new age.[22]

In fact, two recent philanthropic contributions to universities are notable for their "transdisciplinary" focus on academic research and areas of business and industry. Robert Day, chairman of Trust Company of the West and a Claremont alumnus, donated $200 million in 2007 to Claremont McKenna College for research in finance. And George Lucas, creator of the Star Wars saga and founder of Lucasfilm, gave $175 million in 2006 to the School of Cinematic Arts at his alma mater, USC, where, Lucas said, "I discovered my passion for film and making movies.[23]

The Lucas gift in one sense follows a proud tradition of philanthropy among entertainment industry luminaries in Southern California who have contributed to cultural landmarks, such as the Los Angeles Music Center and Disney Concert Hall, and to medical research, notably the donations of Lew and Edie Wasserman to the Jules Stein Eye Institute at UCLA and of music producer David Geffen to UCLA for medical research. But in another sense, the Lucas gift recognizes a reality that he helped bring about with the innovations of his studio and his epic films: the rapidly changing, multidisciplinary nature of the entertainment media industry today. "Multimedia has become an important 21st-century vernacular that must be understood and embraced," Lucas said in making his donation. The next chapter examines the entertainment business, Southern California's emblematic art form and founding industry, as it undergoes a technological and global transformation.

7 Entertainment Industry in the Global Media Age

It used to be that Hollywood's product was movies, made by movie studios, exhibited in movie theaters. But digitization has changed everything. Now stuff is being created for cell phones.

Martin Kaplan,
director, Norman Lear Center, Annenberg School for
Communication, University of Southern California

THE ENTERTAINMENT INDUSTRY, which began in Los Angeles one hundred years ago, is facing enormous changes in technology and the global marketplace. "Entertainment content is changing shape," says Martin Kaplan, director of the Norman Lear Center at the University of Southern California. "Imagery is not just TV and movies today. It's in small bites—even ring tones on cell phones. And national borders mean nothing."[1] In one sense, this is nothing new, of course. Over the decades, the industry has weathered repeated turns of technology and spread American movies, television shows, music videos, Internet games, and all other forms of media throughout the world. International motion picture revenues—about $27 billion in 2007—long ago passed domestic receipts, which were just less than $10 billion that year.[2]

Imagination drives adaptation, you might say. The industry adapted to all of these changes because, in simplest terms, its product is narrative and storytelling—which the industry prosaically calls "content." Narrative and storytelling have always taken different forms in different times. So, there is a sense that the changes brought on by digitization, which turns all entertainment into "ones" and "zeros" of computer code, and the distribution of those forms by the Internet will work out all right for the business.

Entertainment is a formidable industry. In Southern California, it employs more than three hundred thousand people in what the Los Angeles County Economic Development Corp. calls a conservative figure because it does not include legions of lawyers, consultants, financiers, and individuals in other trades serving the industry.[3] Its effect on the economy is almost inestimable because "Hollywood" is an imaginative location more than a geographic one and contributes mightily to tourism, artistic endeavor, technical brilliance, and plain dollars-and-cents deal making.

Still, there is concern in many corners of the industry that the world is spinning out of control. The new media seem too easily downloaded, duplicated, pirated. The spectacle of people making videos of themselves and flashing them onto the Internet has many in the business nonplussed. Then there is the historical fact that changes in technology, while ultimately beneficial, have always brought fresh competition. The movie studios of Samuel Goldwyn and Louis B. Mayer, William Fox and Darryl Zanuck didn't pioneer radio and thus didn't foresee television. That was a New York thing that was led by David Sarnoff, William Paley, and Leonard Goldenson. They in turn were outpaced by Ted Turner and cable TV. Walt Disney alone succeeded in all forms of entertainment and invented new ones. Today, his corporate heirs are extending that legacy in new media. Other large companies have adapted by absorbing newcomers. And Hollywood has succeeded over the span of a century by rewarding entrepreneurial spirits and finding ways to give the public stories it wants to see and hear.

In this chapter, I explain trends and directions of the industry through examples of companies small and large as they have created and adapted to innovations in media and the expanding horizons of the global market. Narrative and storytelling still are the unifying themes of the business, as they have been from the times of Homer and the writers of the Bible. And Southern California is still the home of the business, as it has been since 1910 when David Llewelyn Wark "D. W." Griffith made *In Old*

California—a short film, in Hollywood, a village about five miles from the town of Los Angeles.

But that's not to say it is business as usual. On the contrary, the Internet and the ever-widening global economy are transforming the industry. For one thing, audiences today do not simply watch or hear stories; they participate in the narratives by taking on a persona or character in an Internet game or drama. "We have millions of people taking on roles in our Pirates Website," Robert Iger, president of Walt Disney Co., told a luncheon audience recently.[4] He was referring to the complex multimedia presentation of its *Pirates of the Caribbean* saga as movie, digital video, Internet game, virtual reality series, and online store for costumes and merchandise. At the time, he said the company was still in the process of working out the "business model" for these new media.

More Than a Game

Elsewhere, business models for new media are fast emerging as companies grow into global giants. For an understanding of the far-reaching implications of these phenomena, we begin with video games—where entertainment media melds into the big industrial economy and vice versa. Only yesterday, video games were seen mainly as computer pastimes for teenage boys. But now, games are the valuable properties of major corporations, as an international business deal late in 2007 amply demonstrated. Vivendi of France and Activision Inc. of Santa Monica agreed to a merger deal valued at $19 billion to create Activision Blizzard, a new company that owns highly successful game franchises. Activision Blizzard combines the *Guitar Hero* series, in which players participate in videos of rock bands, and Vivendi's *World of Warcraft*, an online competition that has more than 9 million players worldwide.[5] The new company will take in about $3.8 billion in game sales per year, about the equal of games industry leader Electronic Arts, the publisher of *Madden Nfl* and other sports games. Still, the fact that games have become big business is less significant than the ways in which they blend a virtual world with the physical one. USC's Martin Kaplan offers an arresting example, citing Vivendi's game. "*World of Warcraft* is a 'massively multiplayer game,' meaning that simultaneously millions of people all over the world are online playing that game," Kaplan told me in 2006. "And because you can win coins in the game, you can sell your coins to other players who want to accumulate winnings. So, there is a village in China that has gone from an agricultural economic base to one in which villagers play the game for coins because they can sell the game coins on eBay for real money." The game is bringing in more money than farming, Kaplan says, "and that is just a hint of the astounding changes occurring in media." In fact, what Kaplan describes is but one aspect of a phenomenon called "gold farming" that was described in an article in the *New York Times Magazine.* Turning virtual coins into real currency is in some cases a highly organized business in China, with employees earning the equivalent of 30 cents an hour to play the game, then turning over their virtual money to a foreman who delivers it to a wholesaler who then trades it in a distribution system for real currency from the United States and Europe. The whole business certainly is, as Kaplan says, a hint of the "astounding changes occurring in media."[6]

The changes also are astonishingly rapid, considering that commercial traffic on the World Wide Web dates only to the early 1990s—specifically to a Superhighway Summit meeting at UCLA in 1994 that brought together industry, government, and academic leaders. A decade and a half later, 13.7 million people subscribe to Second Life, an elaborate Website that was created in 2003 by Linden Research, Inc. (Linden Lab), a San Francisco company. In a way, Second Life is a virtual version of "playing house," with participants taking on roles in communities and real companies establishing offices, factories, and showrooms on the site. Linden Lab describes Second Life as a "3D digital world imagined and created by its residents" that businesses can use to research new product ideas with a community of consumers. IBM agrees. In a 2007 presentation titled "Navigating the Media Divide," IBM's Global Business Services division said that Second Life offers a "walled garden" where consumers "form relationships with advertisers and brands" and can purchase products in a virtual world and have them delivered to their homes in the real world.[7] The implications obviously are profound for the advertising and marketing industries. One only has to look at a few statistics to see a direction the ad business is taking. Advertising on the Internet, which often accompanies information searches and entertainment offerings, rose in the U.S. market from $1.65 billion in 2002 to a projected

$16.7 billion in 2009, according to PricewaterhouseCoopers' "Global Entertainment and Media Outlook." And total advertising expenditure in China soared from $31.4 billion in 2002 to $115 billion in 2008 and a projected $132 billion in 2009.[8] Internet media comprise more than half of China's totals.

Further adaptations of virtual realities are developing constantly. The Defense Department, for example, has worked with USC's Institute for Creative Technologies and Hollywood companies since 1999 to produce military training videos. James Korris, a writer and producer of television shows, worked with the military for seven years at USC. "The army wanted narrative and storytelling in their digital productions," Korris says. The result, in such videos as *Full Spectrum Command* and *Full Spectrum Leader*, went well beyond simple war games. "Even the most sophisticated games are just 'first shooter' stories—you shoot other guys and take their stuff," Korris says. "But in a video for training squad leaders, you have to deal with ideas and interpersonal skills as well as the realities of urban battle sequences in places like Iraq."[9] Korris's company, Creative Technologies Inc., still works with the army designing advanced videos and also works with Boeing, Lockheed, and other defense contractors to bring "narrative and storytelling" to military strategy productions. The bottom line: Hollywood in the Internet age is no longer an exotic corner of the U.S. economy but part of the industrial mainstream.

Abundant opportunities come with that status. Southern California for the first time is emerging as a focus of venture capital because it is home to the entertainment industry. "We're seeing the nexus of Internet technology with the entertainment industry," a business analyst at PricewaterhouseCoopers observed.[10] New profit from unimagined sources is already visible. The accounting firm Deloitte & Touche reports that people using cell phones to send text messages, at twenty cents a pop, produce more revenue each year (for cellular phone providers) than the entire global music business.[11] Private equity capital also is flowing into Los Angeles to invest in making motion pictures because the Internet promises dramatic reductions in distribution costs. "We're seeing investors raise specialized mutual funds to back productions of a dozen to two dozen movies," says John Loncto, a Los Angeles attorney who does the legal work on such packages at Greenberg Traurig, an international law firm. "The thinking is that if they back a variety of projects, they will participate in a few global blockbusters."[12]

To capture the magnitude of the Internet revolution in media, we must look at the evolving world of social networking Websites such as MySpace and Facebook and search engines such as Google and its Chinese challenger, Baidu. MySpace is an online social networking site that features self-generated profiles and Web logs (blogs) of more than 200 million members worldwide, plus downloaded music and chat rooms. It was created in 1998 by Chris DeWolfe, a student at USC's Marshall School of Business, and Tom Anderson, a student at UCLA, and has proved to be a pioneer of user-generated content. When members join, they enter a profile of themselves, state their likes and dislikes, say who they would like to meet, etc. The Website became a place for young people to share thoughts and form networks of friends. Note well: MySpace didn't offer its own storytelling; the stories were those of the members conversing with each other—hence *user-generated content*. DeWolfe did offer one attraction by putting the music of little-known bands online. Some bands, when they became famous, never forgot the early break from MySpace and continue to preview their music on the site, which now includes the music of more than eight thousand bands. The bands attract more members and profiles to MySpace. The commercial attraction of this was obvious to Geoff Yang, of Redpoint Ventures, a leading venture capital provider, who invested $11.5 million in MySpace's parent organization, Intermix Inc., in 2004—when MySpace had only 1 million members. Yang's reasoning was that MySpace's information held great value for advertisers, who could pinpoint messages to individuals rather than broadcasting to nonspecific groups. "The site becomes a way for advertisers to reach young people who don't like to be shouted at or marketed to," Yang told me in 2006.[13]

Part of the Experience

A media giant also was attracted to MySpace. In 2005, after MySpace's membership had grown to 24 million, Rupert Murdoch's News Corp. bought Intermix for $580 million. Ross Levinsohn, a media executive who helped make that acquisition for News Corp., later explained that

Murdoch and other Fox executives "felt that media consumption was changing—especially among the under-thirty set." So they formed Fox Interactive Media in early 2005 to gather online sites and then bought Intermix—but quickly sold that company's other Websites to concentrate on MySpace. "What was really interesting to us was that MySpace provided a platform, and kids happily offered up all sorts of information about themselves. A certain demographic wants to be part of the experience, not just sit back and watch what traditional media pushes on them," said Levinsohn in a 2006 interview.[14] MySpace, now headquartered in Fox Interactive's Beverly Hills offices, continues to lead among social networking Websites, with 70 million visitors a month. And DeWolfe expresses confidence. "This is just the beginning of MySpace's evolution," DeWolfe said in a 2007 News Corp. press release. "We're excited to see continued growth and engagement among our users, whether uploading video, registering to vote, or catching up with friends. MySpace continues to be a central part of people's lives."

Amid all the talk of user-generated content and memberships and advertising seeming to grow effortlessly, we should keep in mind that new media does need employees behind the scenes making Websites dance. MySpace had 150 employees when News Corp. bought it, and has considerably more now. A successor company to Intermix, called Demand Media, has 300 employees in Santa Monica and provides a good illustration of how revenues and profits are generated in the new media field. Demand Media was founded in 2006 by Richard Rosenblatt, the man who sold Intermix to Murdoch in 2005. Rosenblatt bought some of the Intermix Websites that News Corp. discarded. He did so with some of the $220 million in venture capital that William Woodward of Anthem Venture Partners raised for him. The Websites that Demand Media has acquired are what Rosenblatt calls "magazines"—sites for particular interests. For instance, the company owns Trails.com, aimed at hiking enthusiasts, and Runtheplanet.com for runners. Demand Media now has fifty Websites, mostly based on user-generated content, with some professionally prepared articles and material added. Here's how it works. "For Trails, a lot of the content will come from hikers themselves, posting information on good hiking areas, changes seen on recent hikes, other tips, and thoughts about places and accommodations," Rosenblatt told me in 2006. Trails.com will pay for articles and material from professional travel and outdoors writers, but the costs of such material could be quite small. "The author might get paid a stipend but could earn more if there are a lot of online visitors to the article," Rosenblatt says. The underlying point of the whole business is that each reader/ hiker/customer can be counted precisely; each view of the Website can be numbered. Fees and advertising payments, therefore, can be made on a per-customer basis. Demand Media also commissions entertainment professionals to make two-minute videos on specific subjects, such as motorcycle riding and beauty pageant competition. The producer gets paid relatively little but can profit from the number of online visits the videos attract. And Demand Media can further control costs by using a service of Google called Google AdSense to steer advertisers to the Websites. The search engine giant earns a fee from advertisers for every prospect contacted through, say, Trails.com—and so does Rosenblatt's Demand Media. How much can such fees be? Perhaps less than a nickel per potential customer. Fees often are based on how much commerce results directly from the ad, as when a prospect buys hiking gear online after clicking on an ad on the Trails Website. Welcome to the new world of pay for results and pay for performance. "It's a business of nickels and dimes that adds up to big money," says Anthem Venture's Woodward. Demand Media, little more than a year old in 2007, reportedly achieved $100 million in revenue and $30 million in profit.[15]

Of course, when new businesses are so attractive, competition increases everywhere. MySpace is hardly alone in the social networking Website world. In South Korea, a community site called Cyworld holds sway among social networking Websites with 24 million members; in Brazil and India, the Google-owned Orkut is the name that attracts 120 million—some 64 million in Brazil and 20 million in India, according to 2008 figures. Friendster, headquartered in San Francisco, is big in Southeast Asia, with more than 70 million users. Facebook, founded in 2004 by a Harvard student, now has 90 million members and has attracted $280 million from investors, including $240 million from Microsoft. YouTube, a site where members can share videos, has become a communications medium unto itself, with candidates for president agreeing to debate for YouTube audiences. Google owns YouTube, having paid $1.65 billion for it in 2006. LinkedIn is another fast-rising site, backed by Sequoia Capital and prominent Silicon Valley investors. LinkedIn concentrates on jobs and hiring and business connections and has 25 million members as of September 2008.[16] New media, in short, is a wide-open field. Even Google, which has become a household word (and a verb—"to google") and a global giant in little more than a decade, is challenged in China, and possibly other countries, by Baidu, a search firm created by two Chinese nationals and backed by global investment bankers.

Ah! China—the enormous market beckoning every media company with visions of millions of customers ready to absorb American output. A glimpse of the Baidu company Website hints that the vision is flawed. The word *Baidu*, the company explains, was inspired by a poem written more than eight hundred years ago during the Song Dynasty, and means literally "hundreds of times," but the word "represents persistent search for the ideal." The corporation "chose a poetic Chinese name because it wants the world to remember its heritage. As a native speaker of the Chinese language and a talented engineer, Baidu focuses on what it knows best—Chinese language search."[17] Sure, the company is touting its own competitive strong suit. But it is also sending a blunt message to Southern California's entertainment media industry: go local to go global. The old business of distributing American movies and shows to foreign audiences now must labor to produce original content for domestic markets like India and China.

Not a Global Village, but a Global Network

And indeed, that message has been heard by Murdoch, whose News Corp. circles the globe with movies, television, sports, and news. In this light, Murdoch's recent activities offer a perspective on media trends. In 2007, News Corp. paid $5 billion to acquire Dow Jones & Co., publisher of the *Wall Street Journal*, and simultaneously launched the Fox Business Network, proposing to invest $300 million to build up a global audience. Murdoch explained his rationale for the investments to *Fortune* magazine: "There's this constant growth of wealth. You have 100 million people joining the world economy every year," he said. "This is the biggest development in the history of the planet almost—the speed at which this is happening.

And while there certainly will be bumps, it's going to go on for another 30 years. Living standards everywhere are going to be better."[18]

Assuming that living standards are rising, Murdoch recognizes that the demand for business information will continue to grow exponentially in developing economies like China and India. PricewaterhouseCoopers, in its latest quadrennial survey of the global outlook for entertainment and media, reports that the market for business information is growing 6 percent a year worldwide but 14 percent a year and more in China and India.[19] This is a clear opening for the *Wall Street Journal*, which is a premier brand lending credibility to business information delivered by satellite broadcast or Internet transmission or simply through the old-fashioned newspaper to any community in the world. Roger Ailes, the communications executive who is heading Murdoch's Fox Business venture, told *Fortune* that "once the *Wall Street Journal* gets integrated" into the company's television and Internet combinations, "we'll ultimately command the world business market."[20]

Other media moguls see a golden harvest in China's millions. Sumner Redstone, chairman of National Amusements and majority owner of Viacom—which owns MTV—boasted to me in 2002 that "the President of China, Jiang Zemin, traveled five hours to see me during my recent trip to Beijing. He called me a musical ambassador" because MTV beams Chinese popular music to 400 million homes in China.[21] But a major aspect of Internet commerce is that a business does not have to be large. Small companies may succeed if they make the effort to build up their presence in a foreign country—particularly in the case of China. The example of AOB Media, a small company in Pasadena and Beijing, speaks volumes. In February 2007, just before the Lunar New Year celebrations in China, AOB Media produced two musical shows in Las Vegas that featured prize-winning Chinese singers, the international star Jackie Chan from Hong Kong, major American rap music stars Kanye West and Gnarls Barkley, and a leading singer from Taiwan. The shows were recorded in Vegas and then shown for six nights all over China by Hunan TV, a satellite service that reached 600 million people. The shows were then converted to programming for distribution throughout China on cell phones and personal computers. The venture was a great success, and AOB Media is producing similar extravaganzas for Lunar

New Year celebrations in 2008 and for the next three years. It was the kind of Chinese and American collaboration that one would think was put on by a multinational giant working with government ministries in China and the departments of state and commerce in the United States. But AOB Media has only 25 employees in Pasadena and connections to 120 employees in Beijing. The company was built on the entrepreneurial energy of Nelson Liao, who emigrated from Taiwan to the United States in the 1980s to get an MBA and then went to China in 1990 as a marketing representative for U.S. pharmaceutical companies. In China, he got into a joint venture in construction materials with a Chinese state-owned company named Citic. That changed his status in an interesting way, Liao told me in 2007. "From that time, the Chinese say I'm a real person," he said. "Before that, they say, 'You're not real because you're a briefcase company—you can run away anytime.' They want you to commit to a long-term relationship."[22]

Liao then cemented that relationship by raising money in the United States to lend to entrepreneurial firms in China. And in 1994 in Beijing, he met Carrie Wang, who among other business activities managed Chinese entertainment artists. Liao and Wang then began to build a media company that in 2005 incorporated as AOB Media in the United States. Liao worked mostly at the American end, with the help of young entertainment professionals, and Wang did important work in China through her Beijing government contacts. "China will open up to the world's media," Laio told me, "but for right now government control is most sensitive to media." Christian Swegal, a music video director and associate of AOB Media who helped line up the American talent for the Las Vegas show, puts the situation more bluntly. "China is different from most other countries," Swegal said. "It prefers contemporary Chinese music to global pop stars. You don't find American and global entertainers featured on radio and television. Everybody thinks China is a big money market, but that isn't the case." Indeed, the first Lunar New Year show was more a cultural breakthrough than a money-making one. "The show cost $1.3 million to put on," said David McKeon, AOB's executive vice president. And the company managed to break even through a share of ad revenue from Hunan TV and cell phone excerpts. "It was an investment to establish trust," McKeon said.

Aesop's Content

To understand the global prospects and technological promise of entertainment media, the best company to examine is the Walt Disney Co. More than any other in Hollywood, it represents works of the imagination, or "content." The company of Walter Elias Disney, who was born in Chicago in 1901, took film animation to higher levels with some early cartoon characters and then in 1928 created Mickey Mouse, a plucky, proud little character who captivated not only America but the whole world. Disney and his studio animators invented numerous characters, from ducks to hound dogs, and adapted Aesop's fables and fairy tales of the brothers Grimm, making them bright, entertaining cinema masterpieces. Disney reflected and informed the American imagination, writes Neal Gabler in his masterful 2006 biography of Disney, which he subtitled "The Triumph of the American Imagination."[23]

Yet despite enormous global success for his animated movies and short subjects, throughout most of his life, Disney fought a constant battle to raise financing and to achieve distribution for his products. In its early decades, the Disney studio was at the mercy of movie theater owners—often divisions of other studios—which controlled the only outlets for filmed entertainment. Ultimately, however, the artistry and attraction of Disney's content, plus a 1948 antitrust decree splitting theater ownership off from studios and the coming of television, brought Disney great success. Indeed, it may well be that Disney's company succeeded in new forms of media as they came along because Disney concentrated so much on creative content. During the early 1950s, for example, as major studios struggled to adapt to the wonder medium of television, Disney signed an agreement with the American Broadcasting Company (ABC) for programs that would show his firm's unforgettable characters as well as innovations, such as the Mickey Mouse Club, that delighted children. (Much later, decades after Disney died of cancer in 1966, Walt Disney Co. purchased ABC, which remains one of the most profitable operations in Disney's $36-billion-a-year worth of entertainment media attractions.)[24]

Back in the 1950s, revenues from the television programs in turn helped finance one of Disney's greatest creations, Disneyland, which opened in Anaheim in 1955 and transformed the traditional amusement park of Ferris wheels and cotton candy into a much grander invention of the imagination. Disney Worlds and Disneylands have since opened in Orlando, Florida, and in Tokyo, Paris, and Hong Kong. And more are sure to come as the Disney Company expands into themed ocean cruises and vacation resorts attached to theme parks. The point is that as media forms multiply, the Disney Company adapts its features to fit the environment. That's why *The Lion King* is not only a feature film, but also a stage play and a theme park attraction; why *Pirates of the Caribbean* is not only a film series and theme park attraction, but also something very new, an online computer role-playing game that enrolls its audience as participants who take on their own virtual personas in the developing drama. That's why the Disney Company is a beacon to the industry at this time and an ideal model for the twin themes of this chapter: entertainment media as it evolves through technological change and globalization.

Global Markets, New Technologies

Disney is making a major push into emerging markets in China, India, Russia, Brazil, Indonesia, and other countries that now hold potential customers whereas yesterday they were perceived as holding only hungry masses. The company notes that as of 2008, the number of "major entertainment platforms" in China will exceed that of the U.S. market.[25] By "entertainment platforms," Disney means the totals of Internet and mobile phone subscribers and households with digital video and multichannel television and computer capabilities. But Robert Iger cautioned his audience at Disney Company headquarters in Burbank recently that success in such markets would be neither easy nor quick. Disney could not simply dub movies and programs with Mandarin, send them into China, and walk away with the cash. For one thing, China restricts the import of foreign films—rampant piracy notwithstanding. The realities of the market dictate that Disney, the entertainment giant, must become local in China, even as tiny AOB Media had to do. "We are making a film in China, with Chinese personnel," Iger said. "It is a film for the Chinese audience, not initially for global distribution. It may only cost $5 million, but we're not sure we'll make money with it. However, it will help us learn the market and become domestic in it."[26]

The payoff is more certain, however, for all the other media products Disney is feeding into China. The company is adding to the numbers of children in its Dragon Club, the Asian descendant of the Mickey Mouse Club. It reports that *Mickey Mouse Magazine* is the most popular publication for China's youngsters. As its local presence grows, with films and shows made in China, so will it bring in more attractions made abroad and adapted for the huge Chinese market. Similarly, in India Disney is making product locally that adapts ideas perfected in the United States, such as a Hindi-language version of its runaway television hit *High School Musical.* And here's an arresting statistic: the number of people fourteen years of age and younger in India was reported at the beginning of this decade to be greater than the entire U.S. population. Disney is adapting *High School Musical* versions for Latin America and Russia, too. No wonder the company looks for sales and income growth greater than 10 percent a year in such large markets. In truth, these are not *foreign* markets but *future* ones, the key to continued prosperity and job growth for Disney's more than 135,000 employees in Southern California and around the globe. The company now gets 25 percent of its revenues from outside the United States. Iger aims to make that 50 percent by 2012 or so.[27]

Virtual Penguins

The other frontier for Disney and the whole industry is the emerging technology of virtual life, in which the audience creates its own story. "We have the online Club Penguin that kids love," Iger told me in 2007. Club Penguin is a Website developed by Canadian entrepreneurs and acquired by Disney in which children choose a penguin personality of their own and participate in adventures. Even as Disney acquired the club with plans for expansion, Club Penguin had 700,000 subscribers and 12 million players in its first two years. "We plan an online club based on *Cars*, the animated movie feature, as well as *Pirates* and *Fairies* with Tinker Bell," Iger said. Disney Fairies is a virtual world aimed at seven- and eight-year-old girls who choose Tinker Bell–like fairies for role- and game-playing, including shopping for clothes. Virtual shopping has a counterpart in the real world, where sales of Fairies tea sets and Tinker Bell fleece nightgowns reached $750 million in 2007. And in 2009, the Fairies franchise will become a feature film called *Tinker Bell*, continuing the Peter Pan saga, which Disney owns. "The picture will have a guaranteed audience of millions, an instant blockbuster," exclaims Michael Cieply, a journalist and author who has covered entertainment media for three decades.[28]

Indeed, the new media represented by Disney's Fairies and Club Penguin is not child's play but serious business. Yet with all the changes over a century, the entertainment media industry remains a game of imaginative storytelling and entrepreneurial flair. A present-day example of this flair is Trish Lindsay, a young woman from Chicago who started out designing concepts for theme park attractions at Walt Disney Imagineering, a division of Walt Disney Productions. She left there in 2000 to found a toy company, succeeded, and sold that business and cofounded another company in 2002 called Star Farm Productions. This company creates stories for children that can be shown or played in cartoon form on cell phones, TV sets, DVDs, and even in storybooks. It has produced twenty-five features as of 2007, chief among them a series of stories about Edgar and Ellen, Charles Addams–like twins who have adventures with other characters. The series has been translated into twelve languages in sixty-six countries, has TV shows on three continents, and reaches audiences online in 120 countries. For help with distribution, Star Farm has commercial partners in fifteen countries, including Simon & Schuster and Mattel in the United States. "We make the stories for any format and put them out there hoping for distribution," Lindsay says.[29] That's just the way Walt Disney did it when he started out.

Indeed, for farsighted entrepreneurs, this is a time of opportunity in entertainment media. For example, Philip Anschutz, the entrepreneur who built the country's largest fiber-optic cable on the rights of way of the old Southern Pacific Railroad, bought three movie theater companies that were bankrupt in 2001. A native of Kansas, he came to Los Angeles in the late 1990s and built the Staples Center, a premier venue for sports and concerts. He bought interests in professional hockey's L.A. Kings and basketball's L.A. Lakers as well as soccer's L.A. Galaxy and built a soccer stadium in Carson in southeast Los Angeles County. Currently, he is developing a complex of live entertainment theaters, hotels, restaurants, and other attractions called LA Live near the Staples Center, in a formerly nondescript area near downtown Los Angeles. Anschutz, who is credited by *Forbes* as having a net worth of $7.8 billion, also has taken to investing in movies. But he has no ambition to be a Hollywood mogul. Rather, he sees movies, live entertainment, and sports attractions as properties that can be distributed worldwide through Anschutz Entertainment Group's growing ownership of arenas—Staples in Los Angeles plus major centers in London and Berlin—and theaters and sports complexes worldwide.

Anschutz's plan for his six thousand theaters is to tap into the new economics of film and concert distribution via the Internet. To explain: From the earliest days of Hollywood, movies have been distributed to theaters in canisters, shipped via air and truck and train to cities and towns everywhere, and then trundled to other destinations in an antediluvian process that is costly and cumbersome. Technology is changing all that. It is now possible for studios to beam movies via the Internet directly to the theater—or to an arena or even a handheld video device or cellular telephone. The cost reduction is sizable—up to half of the cost of traditional distribution. The process was slow to catch on, however, because most theater owners were reluctant to pony up the $15,000-per-screen cost of adapting to Internet distribution. But adroit lenders and private equity investors worked out ways to provide financing for the transition to Internet distribution, and more theaters are being converted. When those borrowings are paid off in a few years, costs will be coming down for all movie studios.

Meanwhile, Anschutz, having equipped his theaters with the necessary receivers, is now showing operas and musical events in movie theaters around the United States. Anschutz Entertainment Group's long-term ambition, an aide to the press-shy Anschutz explains, is "to be the largest live entertainment company in the world." With concert ticket sales in 2007 of almost $750 million, AEG is close to achieving that status. And the possibilities of the business are only expanding.[30]

The historian Arnold Toynbee in his twelve-volume *A Study of History* measured the rise and decline of civilizations by how societies responded to challenges. In this sense, Southern California's founding industry has been challenged by technological transformation and globalization and has responded by adapting to new possibilities. It is a virtual certainty, to coin a phrase, that entertainment media will expand and prosper in the global economy. But a contemporary Toynbee might well ask how the vast Southern California region that gave rise to the industry will respond to the many challenges it faces in population, transportation, education, environment, and human relations. Will the region truly fulfill its destiny as the center of the global economy? In the next chapter, we consider Southern California's challenge and response.

8   Time to Look Ahead

A world-economy always has an urban center of gravity, a
city, as the logistic heart of its activity. News, merchandise,
capital, credit, people, instructions, correspondence all flow
into and out of the metropolis.

Fernand Braudel, historian

SOUTHERN CALIFORNIA has attained the stature of an
urban world center, as the French historian Fernand
Braudel defines it above and as I've explained in the preceding chapters.
Indeed, Braudel foresaw the rise of the Los Angeles region in a 1981
interview with *Forbes* magazine. When asked whether any new area
embodied the dynamism of the then-emerging global economy, Braudel
pointed on a wall map to the southward-sloping shoreline of Los Angeles
and Orange counties and exclaimed, "It is there, Mesoamerica."[1]

The scholar, who died in 1985, anticipated the shift of the U.S. economy
to the Pacific Rim and the region's central role in the new age. Today,
Southern California's dynamism is more widely acknowledged as contact
and trade with Asia and Latin America propel its economy toward $1 tril-
lion in terms of gross annual product—larger than all but ten countries
of the world.[2] Southern California's great polyglot population, more than
22 million in 2008, also fulfills Braudel's criterion for a world region, that
it be "a Noah's Ark, a scene of fantastic mixtures, whether London, or Is-
tanbul, Isfahan or Malacca, Surat or Calcutta."[3] By 2020 the population
of this region's six counties is expected to grow to nearly 25 million.[4]

Yet for all its current recognition as a place of cultural novelty, new wealth, and ethnic diversity, Southern California is still regarded as a national side issue—in the vanguard, perhaps, but not at the center of American civilization. "Policy and intellectual standards still come from the East, from the Boston–Washington corridor," says California historian Kevin Starr.[5] But that is about to change as Southern California enters a new phase in its development, one that will fulfill its destiny as the American center of the global economy.

Confusion about Southern California arises because it remains extraordinarily decentralized. Los Angeles County's 89 cities, Orange County's 35 cities, San Diego County's 18 cities, all the way up to Riverside County's 159 cities make it difficult for economic analysts to comprehend the area's totality. And the region has undergone a daunting transformation in the past few decades. I have reported on and written about this area for forty years, writing for the *Los Angeles Times* and *New York Times* about business and the economy in California and the West. When I began to write about the region in 1969, the great growth spurt of the 1950s and 1960s had brought new prominence to Southern California. Chancellor Franklin Murphy had pushed UCLA to a position of academic and cultural influence equal to any such institution in the United States. UC Irvine, founded in 1965, was still in its startup phase, and UC San Diego was less than a decade old and years away from the prominence in medicine and engineering it enjoys today. Murphy had served UCLA for eight years and had moved over to be chairman of the Times Mirror Corp., the Chandler family company that owned the *Los Angeles Times* and was *the* power center of the local economy.[6]

It was still an old-style economy, led by a few large companies and banks that were managed by a handful of prominent men, known in Los Angeles as the Committee of 25. Yet within two decades that old-style structure practically vanished and was replaced by the entrepreneurial, decentralized economy we know today. "You didn't have a lot of entrepreneurs in those days," Richard Riordan reflected in a 2006 retrospective on the region. "Today we have an overabundance of entrepreneurs."[7] Riordan helped transform the economy by founding two companies in the 1980s that financed entrepreneurial ventures. He also founded a law firm and served as mayor of Los Angeles from 1993 to 2001.

In the preceding chapters I have described the region's transformation to an economy led by international trade and entrepreneurial energy, by new people from Latin America and Asia, and by technological innovation in its universities and information industries. During the early years when those changes were occurring, I was told repeatedly by ostensibly sage businesspeople that the region would "never recover" or would "never be the same." They meant this as a negative, but as the preceding chapters have shown, "never being the same" has turned out to be the region's salvation.

Challenges Formidable

Now, it is time to look ahead, to a vision of the next decade and beyond. Sure, its a tough time for vision with the economy in recession. But present clouds do not banish future promise. This region's economy and stature are primed to blossom, spurred by the expansion of trade and contact with Asia and Latin America and by the enterprise of new people and their offspring. This region will be recognized as the reflection of a new America, the renewal of *e pluribus unum*—"out of many, one"—for the twenty-first century. But the challenges are formidable. Southern California must make sure that it expands the physical infrastructure—the means of transportation, the port and airport facilities, new systems to ensure the availability of water—to accommodate economic expansion. More important, it is imperative that the region improve the human infrastructure—the education of its children, the political and social melding of its diverse peoples—to form a dynamic and thriving society.

The challenges are specific and urgent. To begin with, traffic congestion has made the word *freeway* a misnomer much of the time (see Figure 8.1). According to a study in the *Los Angeles Times*, the economy of greater Los Angeles loses $12 billion a year in foregone output due to traffic congestion, and other counties experience similar frustrations.[8] Indeed, Orange and Los Angeles counties estimate that their citizens spend seventy-two hours a year sitting in delayed traffic—twice the amount of time lost to congestion in the early 1980s. There are plans to remedy the situation, to be sure. In Los Angeles, several major light rail transportation projects are underway, as are improvements to the International Terminal at Los Angeles International Airport. In Orange

Figure 8.1. Typical traffic congestion on Interstate 405, both directions, near the Wilshire Boulevard and Montana Avenue exits. Photo by Lawrence Ho. Reproduced by permission of the *Los Angeles Times*.

County, John Wayne Airport is undergoing at $650 million expansion, and the county is spending $2.5 billion to improve commuter rail service. In San Diego, county government is moving ahead with a $650 million improvement and expansion of the Lindbergh field Airport.[9]

Then there is the compelling need to expand and environmentally clean up the port complexes. The ports of Los Angeles and Long Beach have mushroomed in size and importance during the past decade as the U.S. economy has opened to Asia. Fortunately, billions of dollars have been invested in the port complex year by year to keep pace with the demands of U.S. importers for goods from China, Japan, Korea, and other Asian nations. But the long-term growth of Asia will exert pressure for a further expansion and adaptation of the Southern California logistics systems. Indeed, the Los Angeles County Economic Development Corp. estimates that within five years the ports will be forced to operate twenty-four hours a day, seven days a week, to handle the flow of goods.

So the ports of San Pedro Bay, as the joint facilities are now being called, have embarked on a $2.2 billion Clean Air Action Plan that will reduce emissions in the harbor area by 45 percent by 2011.[10] Such environmental reform is necessary not only for its own sake but to respond to voter outcries about polluted air that could result in legislation to severely limit the ports' operation. As cargo volumes increase, other facilities will have to be built as well—better roads and railroads, loading docks, and warehouses. Economist John Husing, who analyzes the regional economy from a base in San Bernardino, estimates that doing the job right for Southern California's trade and logistics infrastructure will demand $36 billion of investment—including $10 billion for environmental mitigation.[11] There are also major challenges to ensure the availability of water to Southern California at a time when allocations from the Colorado River and northern California are being cut back. Ten projects for desalinating ocean water are on the drawing board in the region. So bills for infrastructure are coming due.

But those bills are arriving just when there is almost no money for public works. The California state budget is in deficit, city budgets are in deficit, and the federal budget is in deficit. Yet I believe that the challenges will be met and progress will come about. And I'm not alone. "There is no money in government, so infrastructure projects will be accomplished through public-private partnerships," former California governor Gray Davis said to me in 2008.[12] "CalPERS will invest in infrastructure," Davis said, referring to the California Public Employees' Retirement System, the nation's largest public pension fund, with more than $240 billion in assets. As CalPERS and other pension funds invest in infrastructure projects, they will be joining a trend. Nationally, Warren Buffett's Berkshire Hathaway Inc. is investing in infrastructure projects; and Macquarie Group, a giant Australian firm, sees great opportunity in investing in U.S. infrastructure.

Tolls for Freedom

If freeways are clogged, making them less "free" might help unclog them. David Fleming, a Los Angeles lawyer and chairman over many years of commissions on public works and government programs, suggested at a 2008 panel discussion that charging tolls on highways is essential if the necessary roads are to be built. "The roads were never 'free' anyway," he noted. "They are paid for in gasoline taxes. If tolls allow speedier traffic, they can be a public benefit." Fleming suggested, for example, a widening and extension of a highway north of Los Angeles County that could carry truck traffic to San Bernardino and Riverside counties without adding to the congestion in the metropolitan core.[13] Charging tolls would allow the road to be built, conferring an economic benefit from more efficient transportation, and would pay back its cost over time. The same goes for expansions of ports and other infrastructure, says economist Husing. "You borrow and then you build and you institute a user fee to repay the debt," he says, referring to user fees on shipping containers and tolls on roads. Indeed, one of the first Clean Air Action Plan decisions, in 2007, was to charge shippers a small fee of $35 per fully loaded container to finance the purchase of lower-emissions trucks. Another $15 fee was tacked on to finance six-lane highways to speed cargo from the ports.

Such investment will pay returns many times over, Husing says, in "a potential 1 million additional jobs." Keep in mind, he adds, "that jobs in goods movement are the kind we need, good-paying blue-collar jobs that employ the 44 percent of the population that does not go to any college." More than traditional stevedoring jobs are involved also, as there is a growing technological quotient to logistics development at the region's seaports and airports. Thanks to security requirements after 9/11, advanced communications and sensor systems now monitor the content of containers and cargo holds. Rail systems have been automated, and there are experiments with magnetic levitation and other technologies for moving freight. All of these developments are linked to federally financed projects at California State University, Long Beach, which has created a marine sciences research center to work on technologies of goods movement, inspection, transport, storage, and finance that are part of a global industry. "The San Pedro harbor area will become a maritime Silicon Valley," says William Lyte, an engineering consultant who has worked on Southern California's infrastructure for a quarter century.[14]

Airports, too, will have to modernize and expand. Los Angeles International Airport (LAX), which has become the nation's busiest international gateway, is currently investing $1.5 billion to construct another runway and upgrade its facilities. But LAX, which handles 61 million passengers annually, 17 million of them international, cannot grow to accommodate vastly greater numbers. It is simply too small, at 3,425 acres, compared with other major airports, such as Chicago's O'Hare and London's Heathrow, at roughly 20,000 acres each. Those hubs have room to grow; LAX does not. For a time during the 1990s, it was thought that a new international airport would be built at the former El Toro Marine Corps Air Station in Orange County, but local voters rejected that possibility. So the future development of air travel to and from this region will follow a decentralized plan that concentrates on expanded use of Ontario Airport, near the Inland Empire, and also on long-term plans to build a large airport at Palmdale in north Los Angeles County. LAX will specialize as the international gateway while other traffic is channeled to Ontario and other airports in San Bernardino and Riverside counties. Ontario, for example, is expected to grow from 7 million to 17 million passengers within a decade. Cargo traffic will increase sixfold to 3 million tons annually, relieving the burden on LAX, which now takes 2 million tons of cargo. In fact, given the poor state of public budgets, local officials are discussing selling Ontario Airport to private interests to facilitate expansion financing for LAX. Major international airports, including London's Heathrow, are privatized, and the U.S. Department of Transportation has a program to encourage the study of private financing. Midway Airport in Chicago has been privatized.

In this region, San Bernardino International Airport, on land of the former Norton Air Force Base, opened for passenger traffic in 2008. In Riverside, the March Air Reserve Base has opened civilian cargo service, and expanded use of the base's long runways is under consideration. Additionally, a privately financed commercial cargo facility, called the Southern California Logistics Airport, is operating at Victorville in the high desert area of the Inland Empire. Entrepreneur Dougall Agan has won support from the Department of Transportation, which sees great future volumes of Asian trade moving through a corridor from Los Angeles to the Inland Empire and on to the rest of the United States.[15]

The New Empire

Note that many of the region's future expansions are slated for the counties east of Los Angeles and Orange. Over the next two decades, Riverside and San Bernardino counties—which are as large in area as the New England states—are expected to grow almost 50 percent in population, to 6.5 million. The projection for San Diego County is 23 percent, to about 4 million.[16] With movements of population on that magnitude, decentralization allows flexible responses to change. And the further message in all the planning and building is that the region is coping with its growth. Often-heated arguments over the environment, land use, and residents' preferences are regularly settled by compromise, and communities move on.

Indeed, during the next decade, the image of Los Angeles and all of Southern California as "suburbs in search of a city," as Dorothy Parker once described the area, will change to urban societies built along transportation corridors of mass transit. In downtown Los Angeles, which for most of the 1990s was abandoned to skid row desolation and emptying office buildings, Eli Broad is spurring Grand Avenue, a project worth potentially $3 billion to build new structures and a sixteen-acre park that "will unify the heart of the city from the Cathedral of Our Lady of the Angels down to the Museum of Contemporary Art," as Broad told me in 2003. "It will provide a public center for our city."[17] Broad's project follows a remarkable renovation of downtown Los Angeles in which numerous office buildings are being converted to condominium apartments and public spaces are being reclaimed.

Broad, who came to Los Angeles from Detroit in 1963 to expand his already successful homebuilding firm and later created an investment firm for retirement savings, has been a protean donor to universities, cultural institutions, and elementary and high schools in Los Angeles. As such, he joins a local tradition of visionary magnates, including Harry Chandler, Henry Huntington, and Dorothy Buffum Chandler, who created cultural and educational institutions in the Los Angeles area. It is a tradition of philanthropy, focused on education, that is carried on throughout the region. Former mayor Riordan has made a lifelong passion of helping schools through the Riordan Foundation and other learning centers he has founded in Southern California and nationwide. In Orange County, Irvine Co. owner Donald Bren has donated hugely to UC Irvine, Chapman University, Caltech, and other colleges, including UC Santa Barbara, where he endowed an institute for studying water and how to keep it supplied to semiarid Southern California. In San Diego, Irwin Jacobs of Qualcomm is a major force in building UC San Diego to national and global stature as well as many other institutions in the San Diego area, particularly its school systems.

The emphasis on aiding public schools at the elementary and secondary levels is significant in the philanthropy of these people and other business leaders. Broad and his wife Edythe recently gave $23 million to two charter school organizations, the latest contribution among an estimated $300 million the Broad Foundations have given to urban school improvement. One reason for the focus on classrooms is, in a word, *growth*. The population of Southern California is growing and will continue to grow during the next decade, less from immigration than from natural increase. In the coming years, the working population of Southern California will be the children and grandchildren of immigrants. They will be newly established Americans. Inevitably, there will be opportunity and innovation. A younger population is a gift to Southern California, promising a productive future. But schooling will be critical if the coming generations are to realize their potential and therefore the potential of the region. Right now, as with urban school districts nationwide, the picture is a troubled one.

Too Many Dropouts

The Los Angeles Unified School District (LAUSD), with more than seven hundred thousand students, is troubled, with only three quarters of its students graduating from high school, according to California Department of Education statistics. Dropout rates among Latino students are as high as 21.8 percent by grade 12, and African American students have an even higher noncompletion rate of 24.5 percent. Furthermore, racial tension between Latino and African American youths in schools is a big problem. Violent fighting has broken out on two high school campuses, with police called in to restore order and the schools locked down. Los Angeles is not alone in having racial and ethnic problems in urban high schools, and the problems are serious. But even more serious is the effect of disorder and dropping out on young people who are obviously part of the future of Southern California.[18]

Elsewhere in the region, schools do somewhat better. Orange County achieves an overall graduation rate of 91.4 percent, with Latino and African American minority student dropout rates of 10.1 percent and 11.2 percent, respectively. San Diego County's graduation rate overall is 82.2 percent, but dropout rates for Latino students (19.6 percent), African American students (25.4 percent), and Pacific Islander students (21.4 percent) are high. In an economy running increasingly on knowledge work, such statistics are alarming.[19]

But in many ways the evolving picture is better than the stark numbers indicate. Reforms are occurring through a stress on local control of schools. Grouping schools in clusters to provide continuity for students and teachers is one idea being tried, says Liam Joyce, principal of an LAUSD school in Topanga Canyon. "Four elementary schools feed into one high school," Joyce explains, "the idea being that teachers know the students over a long period and continuity can help prevent dropping out."[20] Charter schools are being formed within school districts and independently. Charter schools are public institutions, supported by taxpayers just like all public schools, but they have greater authority to decide teaching patterns and some aspects of curriculum. These are the kinds of schools the Broads and others like Bill and Melinda Gates and leading investors from Silicon Valley are backing in Southern California.

For example, Judy Ivie Burton was a teacher, principal, and school superintendent for thirty-seven years in the LAUSD but now is chief executive of the Alliance for College-Ready Public Schools, a charter organization that since 2004 has opened seven high schools and three middle schools. Burton is collaborating with the LAUSD to help meet massive classroom needs for the area's expanding population. But she has chosen the charter school path because it gives her flexibility to employ her own ideas about improving student performance. Those ideas include "increased instructional time. We do 190 days in the school year, compared to 163 days for L.A. Unified," Burton says. "And we do three two-hour periods, plus study hall, per day compared to six, one-hour periods." Alliance schools are publicly financed but receive philanthropic support from a unique organization called NewSchools Venture Fund.

The NewSchools fund is "a philanthropy held accountable by the rigors of venture capital financing," says John Doerr, who backed businesses such as Amazon Inc. and Google during twenty-six years of venture investing. Nine years ago he started the NewSchools fund to back charter school management companies. "We give education entrepreneurs money to start or to speed up building their companies," Doerr says. Then the fund's staff, led by Theodore Mitchell, a former college president who is now president of the California State Board of Education, monitors the schools' use of the money and the educational results, which must be better than those of large urban school districts. The fund so far has invested more than $200 million in backing charter schools as models of reform for education.[21]

The NewSchools fund, for example, contributed $4.8 million to help Michael Piscal and his Inner City Education Foundation start View Park elementary, middle, and high schools in the poor neighborhoods of South Los Angeles. Piscal was a teacher at one of Los Angeles' highest-rated private schools until 1994, when he decided to try teaching children in an "underserved" neighborhood. Today, with nine schools open and growing, Piscal notes, "we have a waiting list of parents wanting to send kids to View Park." The schools' teachers are not unionized but earn salaries similar to the $40,000-a-year range of teachers in the LAUSD. And View Park teachers can earn bonuses based on the performance of their students. Piscal boasts that the middle school—grades 6 through

8—"has the highest test scores in math for African American students in all of California." Brian Taylor, principal of the middle school, explains that such performance is achieved by concentration on the students. For instance, Taylor says, "If kids are struggling, we pull them out of physical education one day or two a week and give them assistance."

Minority Parents and Business Leaders

A couple of points should be underlined about these new approaches to education in the region. One is that relatively poor parents, mostly in minority groups, are determined that their children get a good education and the chance at a better life. They bring pressure on political leaders, who often lead the efforts at reform, pushing teachers' unions and bureaucratic inertia to change the system. Second, the region's business community is deeply involved in supporting school improvement. Together, parents and business leaders could produce in the years ahead a better elementary education system that is decentralized and innovative, a model for the nation.

With such efforts gathering strength, the outlook is brighter for the area's minority students. Mount St. Mary's College in Los Angeles, a private college primarily for women, reflects the aspirations of minority families. Mount St. Mary's has twenty-five hundred students, 58 percent of whom are first in their families to attend college. Fully 98 percent of its students receive financial aid from state or federal grants. Ethnically, the school reflects its area, with 40 percent of its students Latina, 18 percent Pacific Islander, 10 percent African American, 19 percent white, and 6 percent multiracial. The college trains many young women for nursing, with scholarship donations from major hospital chains like Kaiser Permanente that are looking for future employees. It also trains them for work in business, with women-owned businesses providing internships, and for teaching. Practically every year, students from Mount St. Mary's win competitive grants for graduate study in education from the Rockefeller Brothers Fund. A chief attraction of Mount students for the Rockefeller competition judges is that they want to "go back and teach in my old neighborhood," as Monica Arellano, a recent winner, put it—"to teach kids like me whose parents came here."[22] William Butler Yeats once defined education in a way that applies to Southern California's minority students today: "Education is not the filling of a pail," said the poet, "but the lighting of a fire."

A Diversity Laboratory

Importantly, Southern California is primed to demonstrate the advantages of cultural diversity to the whole United States. This will be a significant contribution to the nation because many regions seem to be caught up in a swirl of angry rhetoric over illegal aliens that veers into hostility toward all immigrants. For the most part, this is not true of Southern California, which has more immigrants than any other region. Early in this decade, Los Angeles County had more foreign-born residents than anywhere in the country—more than 30 percent of its population—and neighboring counties also had high numbers. These percentages have been declining in recent years, as relatively fewer immigrants are coming to the region. But the numbers of diverse peoples in the region's future are arresting when one looks at figures from the state government, which lumps diverse peoples into the categories "white," "Hispanic," "Asian," and "black." For example, by 2010 Los Angeles County is expected to have a mix of 2.9 million people classed as white, 5.1 million Hispanic, 1.4 million Asian, and 870,000 black, according to projections by the California Department of finance. Orange County in 2010 will be closely divided between 1.4 million whites and 1.2 million Hispanics; and by 2020 Hispanics will be the largest ethnic group in Orange County and in Riverside and San Bernardino counties and will constitute about half the population of San Diego County.[23]

So yes, Southern California is ideally suited to teach the rest of the United States about ethnic and cultural diversity. The truth about the region is that it now looks the way America will look in the near future as numbers of immigrants and their offspring increase throughout the country. But this future is not like America's past. The Population Dynamics Research Group at the University of Southern California notes that Southern California's ethnic groups are not ghettoizing over generations as ethnic peoples did in past centuries in New York, Boston, and Chicago. Rather, they are moving up in status and often moving on from their original homes in neighborhoods of Los Angeles and Orange

County to spread throughout the region and neighboring states. And the research found that newcomers these days are on the whole better off than new immigrants and their families during previous decades.[24] To say this is not to deny the hardships of uncertain and low-wage work, and people's struggles to adapt and raise children among street gangs and countless pitfalls. But with all the problems of poor areas, no place in the vast expanse of Southern California is simply a depressed environment, visibly without hope. There is an energy in the region, an imagination in its charities as much as in its innovative businesses. One example is Homeboy Industries, a charity founded by Rev. Gregory Boyle, a Jesuit priest, in East Los Angeles that tries to redeem former gang members by putting them to work in Homeboy small businesses, including printing and selling apparel, baking bread and cakes for restaurants and food stores, and running a café and a landscaping business. Like so much else in this region, Homeboy in a dozen years has become a model studied in the rest of the country.[25]

Then, too, as we've already seen, many of the newcomers to this region and their families do business with relatives and associates in their home countries, a phenomenon that scarcely existed in former times. So one of the clear advantages of diversity lies in commerce; it is good business to be situated in Fernand Braudel's "fantastic mixture," or "Noah's Ark."

One can see the truth of this statement at almost any business dinner in the region these days. A recent banquet of the American-Chinese CEO Society, for example, brought together founders of small companies who had come to Southern California to earn academic degrees and, having achieved them, had gone into business here with links to China. They were joined by American businesspeople who were assisting small companies to gain market access in China and Chinese small firms to gain entrée to the U.S. market. Three hundred people attended the dinner; its purpose was networking more than dining. Similar mixing of business and socializing among groups new to America occurs at events as disparate as a dinner to honor the San Gabriel Valley Council of the Boy Scouts of America, which honors mainly Latino scouts and businesspeople, and a conference of the Indus Entrepreneurs, where investments in India, Pakistan, and the United States are the bill of fare.

There is very little nostalgia at these affairs for home villages in Jiangsu, Gujarat, or Michoacán—the kind of dewy memories that immigrants from other lands in other times indulged in. Rather, the emphasis is on success in the new land and the advantage of connections in the old. For the increasing levels of business being done between the United States, Asia, and Latin America, it is good that Southern California offers a crossroads and comfort zone.

Beyond commerce, the deeper lesson of Southern California's diversity—and that of the United States (with Latinos becoming the largest minority in twenty-seven states in 2008)—is that this diversity is not sparking large-scale confrontation and strife. Even on the bitter issue of illegal aliens, the majority of Southern Californians—and a majority of all Americans—want an immigration solution to be worked out, including paths to citizenship for people who came here to work years or decades ago.[26] Today's arguments are nothing compared with the vicious anti-Asian riots of nineteenth-century Los Angeles or the anti-Mexican prejudice of more recent times. To gauge the current temperature, just glance at the municipal leadership of any of the more than two hundred separately incorporated cities in Southern California. In heavily Asian immigrant cities like San Gabriel, one finds a Gutierrez serving on the city council with a Huang; in Anaheim's city council, a Pringle serves with a Hernandez and a Sidhu. A decentralized abundance of incorporated communities makes for opportunities to run City Hall. And the numbers of officials from new ethnic groups grows with every election, as happened in 2007 when Janet Nguyen, a Vietnamese American, was elected one of Orange County's five supervisors.

For a closer view of Southern California as role model for the United States, look at a signal event that occurred in 2005: the election of Antonio Villaraigosa as mayor of Los Angeles. Villaraigosa is the first Latino mayor of Los Angeles in 133 years, or since the days of ranchero culture in the city, and his election was hailed nationwide as a turning point for Latino political power and cultural acceptance. But compared with the past in the city and region, it was no turning point at all. There was no ethnic or racial abuse hurled in the contest between Villaraigosa and his rival, Mayor James Hahn, no open pitting of Hahn's white ancestry against Villaraigosa's Mexican background. (His father was born in

Mexico, his mother in Los Angeles.) No, to find that kind of racial divisiveness, one would have to look back to the mayoral election of 1969, when Tom Bradley, an African American, lost to Mayor Sam Yorty, who ran an openly racist campaign suggesting that whites would not be safe electing a black man as mayor. Things changed after that, though, and Bradley defeated Yorty in a 1973 rematch and went on to serve five terms as mayor of the city, retiring with honors and affection.[27] He was succeeded by Richard Riordan, who defeated Michael Woo, a Chinese American member of the City Council in the 1993 mayoral race, again without taint of ethnic or racial division. The point is that Southern California takes diversity in stride; indeed, hails it and points to its polyglot, multihued population as an asset. This promises a rich future for the region. A cultural case in point is the new Chinese Garden at the Huntington Museum in Pasadena (see Chapter 5). Similarly, the Museum of Latin American Art, which opened in 1996 in Long Beach, offers a place for contemporary art from all of Latin America.

The truth about immigration and California and the United States in the future is the same as it was in the past. People do not come to the United States to fail, to be half-hearted. It was not want of passion and commitment that brought them here. It will not be lack of commitment that carries them forward. To sum up the question of diversity and the region's meaning for the entire country, I turn to Kevin Starr, professor of history at USC, former state librarian, and author of ten works about California history. In his 2004 book *Coast of Dreams*, Starr asked, "Would there be a common culture, a common California?" And he answered: "Yes—but it would be on a different model. Interacting cultural identities would affect and flavor each other." Starr points out that Southern California already boasted "Korean-American bagpipe players, Japanese-American surfer dudes, white homeboys, Latinos who did stand-up shtick. Californians were beginning to resemble each other." The implications for the United States, Starr concluded, were clear: "If and when the United States wanted to see and know itself as a successful world commonwealth, an ecumenopolis, all it had to do was to look to California as it remained the coast of dreams."[28] This conclusion is as true today as it will be tomorrow.

Notes

Preface

1. Interview with Darioush Khaledi, April 1996; and James Flanigan, "A Mass of Buying Power," *Los Angeles Times*, April 10, 1996. Copyright 1996 *Los Angeles Times*. Reprinted with permission.

2. Los Angeles County Economic Development Corp., "2007–2008 Economic Forecast and Industry Outlook," February 2007.

Chapter 1

1. World Trade Center Association–Los Angeles County Economic Development Corp., "International Trade Trends & Impacts," May 2007.

2. Milken Institute, State of the State Conference, Briefing Book, October 2006.

3. Ports of Los Angeles and Long Beach, Economic Impact Study, March 2007.

4. Steven P. Erie, *Globalizing L.A.: Trade, Infrastructure, and Regional Development* (Stanford, CA: Stanford University Press, 2004), pp. 50–54.

5. World Trade Center–Los Angeles County Economic Development report.

6. John Husing, in "Multi-County Goods Movement Action Plan," Southern California Association of Governments, May 2007.

7. Author's interview with Larry Keller, June 2006.

8. Author's interviews with Charles Woo and Peter Woo, January 1995 to March 2006; and James Flanigan, "Toying with a Power Play," *Los Angeles Times*, January 25, 1995. Copyright 1995 *Los Angeles Times*. Reprinted with permission.

9. World Trade Center–Los Angeles County Economic Development report; and Flanigan, "Toying."

10. Mattel, Inc., Website, company history, online at http://www.mattel.com.

11. James Flanigan, "No Boundaries to Success in San Gabriel Valley," *Los Angeles Times*, August 27, 2001. Copyright 2001 *Los Angeles Times*. Reprinted with permission.

12. Author's interview with Dominic Ng, October 2006.

13. Testimony to Congressional-Executive Commission on China, "Is China Playing by the Rules? Free Trade, Fair Trade, and WTO Compliance," September 24, 2003, online at http://www.cecc.gov/pages/hearings/index.php.

14. Author's interview with Sufeng Yao, July 20, 2006.

15. Author's interviews with Stacy Sun and Daniel Qian, July 2007; and James Flanigan, "Chinese Want to Cut Slice Going to U.S. Middlemen," Entrepreneurial Edge, *New York Times*, August 16, 2007. Copyright 2007 the *New York Times*. All rights reserved. Used by permission and protected by the copyright laws of the United States. The printing, copying, redistribution, or retransmission of the material without express written permission is prohibited.

16. Author's interview with George Rudes, August 2006; and James Flanigan, "When Jeans Don't fit a Woman Past Adolescence, a Business Is Born," Entrepreneurial Edge, *New York Times*, September 21, 2006. Copyright 2006 the *New York Times*. All rights reserved. Used by permission and protected by the copyright laws of the United States. The printing, copying, redistribution, or retransmission of the material without express written permission is prohibited.

17. Author's interview with Henry Fan, August 2005; and James Flanigan, "A Middleman Who Doesn't Feel Squeezed by China," Entrepreneurial Edge, *New York Times*, September 15, 2005. Copyright 2005 the *New York Times*. All rights reserved. Used by permission and protected by the copyright laws of the United States. The printing, copying, redistribution, or retransmission of the material without express written permission is prohibited.

18. Author's interview with Philip Neal, May 2005.

19. Avery Dennison Corp., Annual Report, 2006.

20. Menlo Worldwide Logistics, online at http://www.con-way.com.

21. Author's interviews with Nicholas Weber and Bill Butler, July 2006; and James Flanigan, "Delivering the Goods," *Los Angeles Times*, April 2, 1997. Copyright 1997 *Los Angeles Times*. Reprinted with permission.

22. Author's interview with Marcelo Sada, May 2007; and James Flanigan, "Ports and Distribution Industry Surge Together," Entrepreneurial Edge, *New York Times*, September 20, 2007. Copyright 2007 the *New York Times*. All rights reserved. Used by permission and protected by the copyright laws of the United States. The printing, copying, redistribution, or retransmission of the material without express written permission is prohibited.

23. See John E. Husing, "International Trade, Blue Collar Workers and the Inland Empire's Future," two-part series, Economics & Politics, Inc., September and October 2005; "Inland Empire Quarterly Economic Report," *Quarterly Economic Report*, January 2007; and "Key Industries Driving Riverside County's Prosperity, San Bernardino County's Economics Development," *Quarterly Economic Report*, January 2007, online at http://www.johnhusing.com.

24. "San Pedro Bay Ports Clean Air Action Plan," April 2007, online at http://www.cleanairactionplan.org.

25. Alan S. Blinder, "Offshoring: The Next Industrial Revolution?" *Foreign Affairs*, March–April 2006, pp. 113–128.

26. Author's interview with P. J. Go, March 2006; and James Flanigan, "Electronic Giants Lend Hand, and Cash, to Start Ups," Entrepreneurial Edge, *New York Times*, April 20, 2006. Copyright 2006 the *New York Times*. All rights reserved. Used by permission and protected by the copyright laws of the United States. The print-

ing, copying, redistribution, or retransmission of the material without express written permission is prohibited.

27. Author's interviews with Dwight Decker, 2005; and James Flanigan, "Now, High-Tech Work Is Going Abroad," Entrepreneurial Edge, *New York Times*, November 17, 2005. Copyright 2005 the *New York Times*. All rights reserved. Used by permission and protected by the copyright laws of the United States. The printing, copying, redistribution, or retransmission of the material without express written permission is prohibited.

28. For a description of the company's FlexNet Operations Execution System, see Apriso Corp. Website at http://www.apriso.com; author's interview with Adam Bartkowski, June 2003; and James Flanigan, "Should We Fear High Pay Job Shift?" *Los Angeles Times*, June 22, 2003. Copyright 2003 *Los Angeles Times*. Reprinted with permission.

29. Los Angeles County Economic Development Corp., "2008–2009 Economic Forecast and Industry Outlook," February 2008.

Chapter 2

1. Stephen Segaller, *Nerds: A Brief History of the Internet* (New York: TV Books, Oregon Public Broadcasting, 1998), pp. 62–63.

2. Los Angeles County Economic Development Corp., Economic Reports, L.A. Stats, 2007, Table C-9: "Business Establishments in Southern California by Employment Size of firm," online at http://www.laedc.org.

3. Compilations from estimates in 1992–95 on loss of aerospace-defense industry jobs. Notably, estimates of two hundred thousand jobs lost in Los Angeles County alone, Ralph Vartabedian, "State Jobs Seen Imperiled by Defense Cuts," *Los Angeles Times*, January 30, 1992; contemporary statistics in overviews by Los Angeles County Economic Development Corp., Economic Reports, Economic Forecast and Industry Outlook, 1993–1994, and subsequent through 2008 and 2009, online at http://www.laedc.org.

4. Clinton remarks in James Flanigan, "Rockwell May Be Pointing Way for Defense firms in a New Era," *Los Angeles Times*, August 16, 1992. Copyright 1992 *Los Angeles Times*. Reprinted with permission.

5. Joan Didion, *Where I Was From* (New York: Knopf, 2003), p. 133.

6. U.S. Census Bureau, *2008 Statistical Abstract*, "Business Enterprise: Establishments, Employees, Payroll," available online at http://www.census.gov/compendia/statab.

7. Los Angeles County Economic Development Corp., Economic Reports, 2008–2009 Economic Forecast and Industry Outlook, July 2008, Table 9: "California Technology Employment," p. 24, online at http://www.laedc.org.

8. For more information on Howard Hughes and Hughes Aircraft/Electronics, see Bruce Elbert, "Hughes Aircraft Remembered," Application Technology Strategy, Inc., online at http://www.applicationstrategy.com; and George J. Marrett, *Howard Hughes: Aviator* (Annapolis, MD: Naval Institute Press, 2004), pp. 97–99.

9. See Simon Ramo, *The Business of Science* (New York: Hill & Wang, 1988), pp. 36–116. Also author's interviews with Simon Ramo, March 2000, July 2001, and

February 2002; and James Flanigan, "TRW Is Strong in High Tech but Wall Street Doesn't See It," *Los Angeles Times*, March 26, 2000. Copyright 2000 *Los Angeles Times*. Reprinted with permission.

10. Segaller, *Nerds*, p. 37.

11. Author's interview with Andrew Viterbi, San Diego, April 2006.

12. James Flanigan, "Cold War's End May Open Doors for Defense Workers," *Los Angeles Times*, November 29, 1989. Copyright 1989 *Los Angeles Times*. Reprinted with permission.

13. Author's interview with Henry Samueli, September 15, 2006.

14. Henry Samueli, "The Broadband Revolution," *IEEE Micro* 20:2 (March 2000), pp. 16–26.

15. Author's interviews with Naser Partovi, April and December 2006.

16. Author's interview with Viterbi, April 2006.

17. "The Future Depends on Innovation," interview with Irwin M. Jacobs, *Design and Test of Computers, IEEE* 22:3 (May–June 2005), pp. 268–279; James Flanigan, "Torpedo That Hit Qualcomm Carried a Message," *Los Angeles Times*, July 12, 1998. Copyright 1998 *Los Angeles Times*. Reprinted with permission.

18. Quoted in Trudy E. Bell, "The Quiet Genius: Andrew J. Viterbi," *The Bent* of Tau Beta Pi (national engineering honor society), Spring 2006, pp. 17–21.

19. Qualcomm Inc., 2007 Annual Report, form 10-K in SEC filings, online at http://investor.qualcomm.com/sec.cfm.

20. Author's interview with Irwin Jacobs, April 23, 2008; Irwin Jacobs, address to the Twenty-One Fund, Grand Del Mar Hotel, San Diego, April 23, 2008.

21. Author's interviews with James Cable and John Groe, April 2006; James Flanigan, "Electronic Giants Lend Hand, and Cash, to Start-Ups," Entrepreneurial Edge, *New York Times*, April 20, 2006. Copyright 2006 the *New York Times*. All rights reserved. Used by permission and protected by the copyright laws of the United States. The printing, copying, redistribution, or retransmission of the material without express written permission is prohibited.

22. Bureau of Labor Statistics, table on labor force statistics from 1982 to 2007, online at http://data.bls.gov; Bureau of Economic Analysis, National Economic Accounts, table on gross domestic product (GDP), online at http://www.bea.gov/national; tables on current dollar GDP from 1990 to 2007.

23. Ben Bernanke, speech to Leadership South Carolina, Greenville, August 31, 2006, online at http://www.federalreserve.gov/newsevents/speech/bernanke20060831a .htm.

24. Bureau of Labor Statistics, "Union Affiliation of Employed Wage and Salary Workers, 2007," January 25, 2008, online at http://www.bls.gov/news.release/union2. t0l.htm. Also data on union membership and employment figures (1973–) linked to online version of Barry T. Hirsh and David A. MacPherson, "Union Membership and Coverage Database from the Current Population Survey: Note," *Industrial and Labor Relations Review* 56 (January 2003), 349–354, available at http://unionstats .gsu.edu.

25. Bureau of Labor Statistics, Table B-1, online at ftp://ftp.bls.gov/pub/suppl/ empsit.ceseeb1.txt.

26. Author's interview with Alvin and Heidi Toffler, December 2006; also Alvin and Heidi Toffler, *Revolutionary Wealth: How It Will Be Created and How It Will Change Our Lives* (New York: Knopf, 2006), p. 260.

27. Author's interviews with Kenneth Kalb, April 2006 and March 2007.

Chapter 3

1. For more information, see James Flanigan, "Blindsided: Orange County's financial Crisis," *Los Angeles Times*, December 11, 1994. Copyright 1994 *Los Angeles Times*. Reprinted with permission.

2. Author's interviews with Linda Griego, 1996; and James Flanigan, "Rebuilding LA One Neighborhood at a Time," *Los Angeles Times*, October 30, 1996, and "Post-Riot Recovery: And Miles Still to Go," editorial, *Los Angeles Times*, December 30, 1994. Copyright 1996 and 1994 *Los Angeles Times*. Reprinted with permission.

3. Author's interview with Michael Milken, June 2004; and James Flanigan, "Reagan Economic Policy Is Enduring Influence," *Los Angeles Times*, June 13, 2004. Copyright 2004 *Los Angeles Times*. Reprinted with permission.

4. Langston Hughes, *Collected Poems of Langston Hughes* (New York: Knopf, 2001), p. 426.

5. Michael Milken, "The Democratization of Capital," *California Lawyer*, July 2000, and "Prosperity and Social Capital," *Wall Street Journal*, June 23, 1999, both online at http://www.mikemilken.com/articles.taf.

6. Author's interview with William Link, April 2008; and James Flanigan, "If It's Eye Care Technology, This Must Be Orange County," Entrepreneurial Edge, *New York Times*, May 15, 2008. Copyright 2008 the *New York Times*. All rights reserved. Used by permission and protected by the copyright laws of the United States. The printing, copying, redistribution, or retransmission of the material without express written permission is prohibited.

7. Stephen Pizzo, "Master of the Knowledge Universe," *Forbes*, September 10, 2001; author's interviews with Michael Milken, May 2007 and April 2008.

8. Author's interviews with Brian Argrett, April 2002 and January 2007; James Flanigan, "Building Inner-City Equity," *Los Angeles Times*, April 21, 2002. Copyright 2002 *Los Angeles Times*. Reprinted with permission.

9. For more information see John Mitchell, "Inspirer Banks on Inner City," *Los Angeles Times*, December 22, 1998; Lee Romney, "Financial Center Brings Hope to Maywood," *Los Angeles Times*, May 16, 1998. Also columns by James Flanigan, including "It's Not the Color of Their Skin but the Spirit of Their Enterprise," *Los Angeles Times*, April 28, 1999. Copyright 1999 *Los Angeles Times*. Reprinted with permission.

10. Author's interview with Mary Ellen Weaver, 1998; Riordan, Lewis & Haden Website at http://www.rlhinvestors.com, case study of Data Processing Resources Inc.; author's interviews with Christopher Lewis, Patrick Haden, and Murray Rudin, 2005; and James Flanigan, "Staffing," *Los Angeles Times*, November 1, 1998. Copyright 1998 *Los Angeles Times*. Reprinted with permission.

11. James Flanigan, "San Diego Offers Lessons on Art of the Comeback," *Los Angeles Times*, July 31, 1996. Copyright 1996 *Los Angeles Times*. Reprinted with permission.

12. Los Angeles County Economic Development Corp., census statistics of companies with one to ninety-nine employees in Los Angeles five-county area plus San Diego County, 2006, online at http://www.laedc.org/reports/LAstats-2007.pdf.

13. Author's interviews with Byron Roth and James Montgomery for James Flanigan, "Despite Downturn, financing Exists for Small Companies," Entrepreneurial Edge, *New York Times*, April 17, 2008. Copyright 2008 the *New York Times*. All rights reserved. Used by permission and protected by the copyright laws of the United States. The printing, copying, redistribution, or retransmission of the material without express written permission is prohibited.

14. Author's interviews with Michael Tennenbaum, 2006; Tennenbaum Capital Partners LLC Website at http://www.tennenbaumcapital.com; James Flanigan, "Private Equity Fuels Growth of Small California firms," *Los Angeles Times*, November 20, 2002. Copyright 2002 *Los Angeles Times*. Reprinted with permission.

15. "Where Do Millionaires Live?" *Wall Street Journal*, May 2, 2007, citing Transaction Network Services, a research firm.

16. Center for Korean-American Studies and Korean Studies, California State University, Los Angeles, News Release, November 22, 2002, and census tables, online at http://www.calstatela.edu/centers/ckaks/census_tables.html (tables on self-employment, government sector, unemployment rate, poverty rate, and naturalization rate); Ivan Light and Edna Bonacich, *Immigrant Entrepreneurs: Koreans in Los Angeles 1965–1982* (Berkeley: University of California Press, 1988), p. 19.

17. Quotations and information relevant to the Korean business community are from the following sources: Author's interviews with David Lee, 2001 and 2005; James Flanigan, "New Roots Nurture Local Trade," *Los Angeles Times*, August 27, 2001 (copyright 2001 *Los Angeles Times*. Reprinted with permission); Flanigan, "Roots in the Far East, Doing Deals in the West," Entrepreneurial Edge, *New York Times*, October 20, 2005 (copyright 2005 the *New York Times*. All rights reserved. Used by permission and protected by the copyright laws of the United States. The printing, copying, redistribution, or retransmission of the material without express written permission is prohibited); author's interview with Charles Rim, 2005; author's interview with Sung Won Sohn, September 2006; author's interview with Stewart Kim, 2003; author's interviews with Sabrina Kay, 2002 and 2006; and James Flanigan, "A Sharp Mind Who Redefines 'Cutting Edge,'" *Los Angeles Times*, January 1, 2003. Copyright 2003 *Los Angeles Times*. Reprinted with permission.

18. Quotations and information relevant to the Vietnamese business community are from the following sources: author's interviews with Hieu Nguyen, Jocelyn Tran, Thinh Nguyen, Paul Nguyen, George Baker, and others in U.S. Vietnamese communities and Vietnam, December 2005; James Flanigan, "Little Saigon Exports Its Prosperity," Entrepreneurial Edge, *New York Times*, January 19, 2006. Copyright 2006 the *New York Times*. All rights reserved. Used by permission and protected by the copyright laws of the United States. The printing, copying, redistribution, or retransmission of the material without express written permission is prohibited.

19. Quotations and information relevant to the Indian business community are from the following sources: author's interviews with Safi Qureshey, Suhas Patil, Sabeer Bhatia, Shivbir Grewal, Apurv Bagri, and others, November 2005; James Flanigan,

various columns, including "India's Tech Economy Shows Promise As It Opens to U.S.," *Los Angeles Times*, March 5, 2000 (copyright 2000 *Los Angeles Times*. Reprinted with permission); Flanigan, "Mutual-Aid Network Links South Asia and U.S.," Entrepreneurial Edge, *New York Times*, December 15, 2005 (copyright 2005 the *New York Times*. All rights reserved. Used by permission and protected by the copyright laws of the United States. The printing, copying, redistribution, or retransmission of the material without express written permission is prohibited).

20. Government of Canada, Canada–U.S. trade and investment partnership, online at http://geo.international.gc.ca/can-am/washington/trade_and_investment/trade_partnership-en.asp.

21. Ronald Takaki, *A Different Mirror: A History of Multicultural America* (Boston: Little, Brown, 1993), pp. 378–385.

22. See James Flanigan, various columns on Japan's economy, *Los Angeles Times*, 1986–2005, including "Only fittest Car Giants Will Survive," August 24, 1988, and "Sony Recharges Its Batteries with an Internet Strategy," May 14, 2000. Copyright 1988 and 2000 *Los Angeles Times*. Reprinted with permission.

Chapter 4

1. Author's interviews with Enrique Hernandez Jr. over eight years; James Flanigan, "Confidence and Innovation Build a Global firm," *Los Angeles Times*, April 18, 1999, and "U.S. Investors Take Wait and See Stance," *Los Angeles Times*, December 3, 2000. Copyright 1999 and 2000 *Los Angeles Times*. Reprinted with permission.

2. Pew Hispanic Center, tabulations of U.S. Census 2000; "American Community Survey," 2005; and "America's Immigration Quandary," March 2006, online at http://pewhispanic.org.

3. Pew Hispanic Center, "Hispanics at Mid-Decade" and "A Statistical Portrait of the Foreign Born at Mid-Decade," August 2006, online at http://pewhispanic.org.

4. Dowell Myers, *Immigrants and Boomers: Forging a New Social Contract for the Future of America* (New York: Russell Sage Foundation, 2007), p. 46.

5. George J. Borjas, *Heaven's Door: Immigration Policy and the American Economy* (Princeton, NJ: Princeton University Press, 1999), p. 190.

6. James M. McPherson, *Ordeal by fire: The Civil War and Reconstruction* (New York: Knopf, 1982), p. 399.

7. Myers, *Immigrants and Boomers*, pp. 65–119; and Aristide R. Zolberg, *A Nation by Design: Immigration Policy in the Fashioning of America* (New York: Russell Sage Foundation, 2006), pp. 293–336.

8. Pew Hispanic Center; see notes 2 and 3.

9. Estimates in this and the following paragraphs by the Federation for American Immigration Reform, "The Costs of Illegal Immigration, 2005," online at http://www.fairus.org; the Center for Immigration Studies, "Immigration's Impact on Public Coffers," by Steven A. Camarota, August 2006, online at http://www.cis.org; and the Pew Hispanic Center, "Statistical Portrait"; and Tamar Jacoby, "Immigration Nation," *Foreign Affairs*, November–December 2006, p. 54.

10. Zolberg, *A Nation by Design*, p. 31.

11. Author's interview with Enrique Hernandez Jr., July 2007.

12. Selig Center for Economic Growth, "The Multicultural Economy," pp. 7–8, online at http://www.selig.uga.edu/forecast/GBEC/GBEC0703Q.pdf.

13. James P. Smith, "Immigrants and Their Schooling," in *Handbook of the Economics of Education*, Vol. 1 (Stanford, CA: Elsevier, 2006), pp. 156–187.

14. Cited in James Flanigan, "Exploding Latino Market Becomes Attractive to Banks," Entrepreneurial Edge, *New York Times*, March 16, 2006. Copyright 2006 the *New York Times*. All rights reserved. Used by permission and protected by the copyright laws of the United States. The printing, copying, redistribution, or retransmission of the material without express written permission is prohibited.

15. Ibid.; and author's interviews with Maria Contreras-Sweet and Hector and Norma Orci, January and February 2006

16. Author's interviews with Emilio Sanchez-Santiago and Jose Akle, 2006; and James Flanigan, "Exploding Latino Market" and "Countering the Big-Bank Trend," Entrepreneurial Edge, *New York Times*, March 15, 2007. Copyright 2007 the *New York Times*. All rights reserved. Used by permission and protected by the copyright laws of the United States. The printing, copying, redistribution, or retransmission of the material without express written permission is prohibited.

17. The material on Cuban business families is drawn from the author's interviews with Gilbert Dalmau, the Rodriguez family, Luis Faura, and the Gaviña family, November 2006; James Flanigan, "A Taste of Cuba in California," Entrepreneurial Edge, *New York Times*, December 21, 2006. Copyright 2006 the *New York Times*. All rights reserved. Used by permission and protected by the copyright laws of the United States. The printing, copying, redistribution, or retransmission of the material without express written permission is prohibited. Also interviews with the Rodriguez family dating back to 1997; James Flanigan, "What Does This Family Business Need?" *Los Angeles Times*, November 14, 2004. Copyright 2004 *Los Angeles Times*. Reprinted with permission.

18. Bank of Mexico statistics and estimates, cited in *Wall Street Journal*, "U.S. Slowdown Hits Mexico As Remittances Drop," July 30, 2008, online at http://www.wsj.com.

19. Estimates from the International Monetary Fund, IMF World Economic Outlook, April 2008, online at http://www.imf.org; and Los Angeles County Economic Development Corp., "Gross Product Comparisons, 2007," July 2008, online at http://www.laedc.org.

20. "Ireland Heads Richest Countries," *The Australian*, August 1, 2007.

21. Author's interview with Gina Quatrine, February 2007.

22. Author's interviews with the Villanueva family in Rustic Canyon/Fontis Partners, June 2006; and James Flanigan, "Latino Funds Help Family Businesses with Posterity in Mind," *New York Times*, July 8, 2006. Copyright 2006 the *New York Times*. All rights reserved. Used by permission and protected by the copyright laws of the United States. The printing, copying, redistribution, or retransmission of the material without express written permission is prohibited.

23. Interview with Norma Orci, January 2006.

24. James Flanigan, "Fighting for Housing," *New York Times*, October 14, 2006. Copyright 2006 the *New York Times*. All rights reserved. Used by permission and pro-

tected by the copyright laws of the United States. The printing, copying, redistribution, or retransmission of the material without express written permission is prohibited.

25. Ibid.; and author's interviews with Oscar De La Hoya and John Long, September 2006.

Chapter 5

1. Los Angeles Economic Development Corp., "International Trade Trends and Impacts: The Southern California Region, 2007 Results and 2008 Outlook," May 2008, online at http://www.laedc.org/reports/Trade-2008.pdf; U.S. Department of the Treasury, "Report on Foreign Portfolio Holdings of U.S. Securities as of June 30, 2007," online at http://www.ustreas.gov/tic/shl2007r.pdf; "China's Forex Stockpile Hits Record $1.8 Trillion," July 14, 2008, online at http://www.marketwatch.com/news/story/chinas-forex-stockpile-hits-record/story.aspx?guid=%7BC54F488B%2D1B7D%2D4F42%2D8846%2D0B5A4F62F254%7D&dist=msr_12.

2. Bureau of Economic Analysis, "U.S. International Trade in Goods and Services, July 2008," September 11, 2008, online at http://www.bea.gov/newsreleases/international/trade/2008/pdf/trad0708.pdf; Asia-Pacific USA Chamber of Commerce cited in James Flanigan, "Chinese Want to Cut Slice Going to U.S. Middlemen," Entrepreneurial Edge, *New York Times*, August 16, 2007.

3. East West Bancorp, Cathay General Bancorp, and Far East National Bank, 2007 annual reports.

4. Author's interviews with Kenneth Courtis, May 2008; and Nomura Research Institute, "Asian Economic Outlook 2003–2004 4th Quarter Report," October 15, 2003, online at http://www.nri.co.jp/english/news/2003.

5. Author's interviews with Donald Tang, 2003–2006, and Tang profile in Notable Names Database, Soylent Communications, 2007, online at http://www.nndb.com/people/865/000120505/.

6. Author's interview with Robert Sweeney, September 2007.

7. Flanigan, "Chinese Want to Cut Slice."

8. Ibid.

9. Ronald Takaki, *A Different Mirror: A History of Multicultural America* (Boston: Little, Brown, 1993), pp. 191–220; Jean Pfaelzer, *Driven Out: The Forgotten War against Chinese Americans* (New York: Random House, 2007).

10. Interview with William Ouchi, Anderson School of Management, University of California, Los Angeles, September 2006; Iris Chang, *The Chinese in America* (New York: Viking, Penguin Group, 2003), pp. 161–162.

11. Author's interview with Gareth Chang, 2006.

12. Author's interviews with Henry Hwang during the 1990s; James Flanigan, "Asian Investment Is Back—More Diverse Than Before," *Los Angeles Times*, September 18, 1996, and "Small Banks See Opportunity in Southern California, *Los Angeles Times*, July 22, 1998; Henry Hwang obituary, *Los Angeles Times*, October 11, 2005. Copyright 1996, 1998, and 2005 *Los Angeles Times*. Reprinted with permission.

13. Author's interviews with Dominic Ng, 1996–2006; and Flanigan, "Asian Investment" and "Small Banks."

14. America Chung Nam, Inc., Website, at http://www.acni.net; and "America Chung Nam Purchases Land," *Los Angeles Business Journal*, April 22, 2002.

15. Author's interview with Roger Wang, May 2006; and James Flanigan, "Building a Business Empire in China," Entrepreneurial Edge, *New York Times*, June 15, 2006. Copyright 2006 the *New York Times*. All rights reserved. Used by permission and protected by the copyright laws of the United States. The printing, copying, redistribution, or retransmission of the material without express written permission is prohibited.

16. Author's interviews with Ng and Tang; and Committee of 100 Website at http://www.committee100.org.

17. Author's interviews with Andrew and Peggy Cherng, 2001 and 2006; Matt Krantz, "Panda Express Spreads Chinese Food across USA," *USA Today*, September 13, 2006; and James Flanigan, "Cooking up a Powerhouse of Chinese Food," *Los Angeles Times*, October 8, 2001. Copyright 2001 *Los Angeles Times*. Reprinted with permission.

18. For more information on Confucius, see Pierre Do-Dinh, *Confucius and Chinese Humanism* (New York: Funk & Wagnall, 1969); and "Analects of Confucius," online at http://www.confucius.org.

19. Author's interviews with John Long, September 2006; and James Flanigan, "fighting for Housing," *New York Times*, October 14, 2006.

Chapter 6

1. Author's interview with Judy Olian, September 2007; and James Flanigan, "Business Schools Break Tradition in Global Education," Entrepreneurial Edge, *New York Times*, February 21, 2008. Copyright 2008 the *New York Times*. All rights reserved. Used by permission and protected by the copyright laws of the United States. The printing, copying, redistribution, or retransmission of the material without express written permission is prohibited.

2. Author's interviews with C. L. Max Nikias, April 2006 and September 2007; and Flanigan, "Business Schools Break."

3. Author's interviews with Andrew Policano, October 2005 and September 2007; and Flanigan, "Business Schools Break."

4. Clark Kerr, *The Uses of the University* (Cambridge, MA: Harvard University Press, 1963), pp. 36–37.

5. Peter Drucker, *Post-Capitalist Society* (New York: HarperCollins, 1993), p. 2.

6. IIE Network (Institute of International Education), *Open Doors* online, 2007 Annual Report, "International Student Enrollment in U.S. Rebounds," "Highlights," "University of Southern California Hosts the Largest Number of International Students," online at http://opendoors.iienetwork.org.

7. Flanigan, "Business Schools Break."

8. Ibid.; and author's interviews with Robert Foster and Elwin Svenson, September 2007.

9. Beckman Foundation Website at http://www.beckman-foundation.com; and James Flanigan, "Southland's Tech Prowess Is in Partnerships," *Los Angeles Times*, March 9, 1998. Copyright 1998 *Los Angeles Times*. Reprinted with permission.

10. Author's interviews with Frederic Farina and Lawrence Gilbert, 2006 and

throughout the previous two decades; and James Flanigan, "The Route from Research to Start-Up," Entrepreneurial Edge, *New York Times*, January 18, 2007. Copyright 2007 the *New York Times*. All rights reserved. Used by permission and protected by the copyright laws of the United States. The printing, copying, redistribution, or retransmission of the material without express written permission is prohibited.,

11. Author interviews with William Otterson, UCSD Connect, February 2005; and James Flanigan, "Biotech Breeding Ground," *Los Angeles Times*, February 15, 1995. Copyright 1995 *Los Angeles Times*. Reprinted with permission.

12. Author's interview with Paul Romer, July 1995.

13. Author's interviews with Erik Viire, December 2006; and Flanigan, "The Route from Research."

14. Author's interviews with Max Nikias and Krisztina Holly, February and August 2006, May 2007; and James Flanigan, "Scientists Turn to the Internet and Venture Capitalists for Backing," Entrepreneurial Edge, *New York Times*, June 6, 2007. Copyright 2007 the *New York Times*. All rights reserved. Used by permission and protected by the copyright laws of the United States. The printing, copying, redistribution, or retransmission of the material without express written permission is prohibited.

15. Author's interviews with Paul Merage and Andrew Policano, 2005; and James Flanigan, "Problem: Good Jobs Are Scarce. Solution: Become Your Own Boss," Entrepreneurial Education, *New York Times*, November 16, 2005. Copyright 2005 the *New York Times*. All rights reserved. Used by permission and protected by the copyright laws of the United States. The printing, copying, redistribution, or retransmission of the material without express written permission is prohibited.

16. Author's interview with Ian Chaplin, October 2006; James Flanigan, "Making Money by Matching Surfers to Marketers," Entrepreneurial Edge, *New York Times*, October 19, 2006. Copyright 2006 the *New York Times*. All rights reserved. Used by permission and protected by the copyright laws of the United States. The printing, copying, redistribution, or retransmission of the material without express written permission is prohibited.

17. Los Angeles County Economic Development Corp., Los Angeles Statistics, Technology Employment, July 2007, pp. 6–11, online at http://www.laedc.org; Ross DeVol and Armen Bedroussian, "Mind-to-Market: A Global Analysis of University Biotechnology Transfer and Commercialization," report for the Milken Institute, September 20, 2006.

18. Author's interview with Albert Carnesale, 2001; James Flanigan, "Science, State, Business Bond in Nanosystem," *Los Angeles Times*, August 13, 2001; and Flanigan, "Nanotechnology—Small Things for Big Changes," *Los Angeles Times*, November 23, 2003. Copyright 2001 and 2003 *Los Angeles Times*. Reprinted with permission.

19. Chih-Ming Ho, "Bio-Nano-Information Fusion," chapter 17 in *Nanotechnology: Science, Innovation, and Opportunity*, ed. Lynn E. Foster (New York: Prentice Hall, 2005), p. 209.

20. Author's interviews with Elena Revazova, Kenneth Aldrich, and William Adams (cofounders of International Stem Cell Corp.), September 2007.

21. Author's interview with Henry Riggs, president, Keck Graduate Institute, June 1997, and Robert Sullivan and Mary Walshok, December 2002; James Flanigan,

"Taking a More Practical Approach to Biomedicine," *Los Angeles Times*, June 18, 1997, "UCSD Business School Will Get Technical," *Los Angeles Times*, December 18, 2002, and "Foreign Funding Blooms for Tech in U.S.," *Los Angeles Times*, April 3, 2004. Copyright 1997, 2002, and 2004 *Los Angeles Times*. Reprinted with permission.

22. Author's interviews with Robert Klitgaard and Ira Jackson, Claremont Graduate University, December 2006.

23. Claremont McKenna College news release, "Alumnus Robert Day Makes $200 Million Gift to Claremont McKenna College," September 27, 2007; USC news release, "Lucasfilm Donates $175 Million to USC," September 20, 2006.

Chapter 7

1. Author's interviews with Martin Kaplan, April and December 2006.

2. Motion Picture Association of America, "Theatrical Market Statistics, U.S. and Global, 2007" and "International Theatrical Snapshot," online at http://www.mpaa .org/researchstatistics.asp.

3. Los Angeles County Economic Development Corp., "2008–2009 Economic Forecast and Industry Outlook," February 2008, online at http://www.laedc.org/ reports/Forecast-2008-02.pdf.

4. Author's interview with Robert Iger, September 10, 2007; and Iger, presentation to the Pacific Council on International Policy, September 10, 2007.

5. Joint press release, Vivendi and Activision, "Vivendi and Activision to Create Activision Blizzard," December 2, 2007; Matt Richtel, "Guitar Hero Gets an Accompanist," *New York Times*, December 5, 2007.

6. Author's interview with Martin Kaplan, 2007; see also Julian Dibbell, "The Life of the Chinese Gold Farmer," *New York Times Magazine*, June 17, 2007, online at http://www.nytimes.com/2007/06/17/magazine/17lootfarmers-t.html.

7. For more information, see http://www.lindenlab.com and http://secondlife .com; Saul Berman, Steven Abraham, Bill Battino, Louisa Shipnuck, and Andres Neus, "Navigating the Media Divide" (IBM Institute for Business Value, IBM Corp., 2007).

8. PricewaterhouseCoopers, "Global Entertainment and Media Outlook: 2007–2012," online at http://www.pwc.com/extweb/pwcpublications.nsf/docid/5AC172F2C9DED 8F5852570210044EEA7.

9. Author's interview with James Korris, December 5, 2007.

10. Quotation from PricewaterhouseCoopers, "MoneyTree Report, 2007," online at http://www.pwcmoneytree.com.

11. Deloitte Touche Tohmatsu, "Technology, Media & Telecommunications Predictions 2007," online at http://www.deloitte.com.

12. Author's interview with John Loncto, November 16, 2007.

13. Patricia Sellers, "MySpace Cowboys," *Fortune*, September 4, 2006; author's interview with Geoff Yang, January 23, 2007.

14. Ross Levinsohn interview with Always On Network, "Murdoch and MySpace," August 27, 2006.

15. Author's interviews with Richard Rosenblatt and William Woodward, 2006

and 2007; James Flanigan, "Making Money by Matching Surfers to Marketers," Entrepreneurial Edge, *New York Times*, October 19, 2006.

16. Rachel Rosmarin, "TheirSpace," *Forbes*, February 12, 2007.

17. "The Baidu Story," online at http://ir.baidu.com.

18. Tim Arango, "Inside Fox Business News," *Fortune*, October 29, 2007.

19. PricewaterhouseCoopers, "Global Entertainment."

20. Arango, "Inside Fox Business News."

21. James Flanigan, "Viacom Shines in a Business That's Getting Bad Reviews," *Los Angeles Times*, September 29, 2002. Copyright 2002 *Los Angeles Times*. Reprinted with permission.

22. Author's interviews with Nelson Liao and other principals of AOB Media, March 2007; James Flanigan, "Let's Put on a Show for China," Entrepreneurial Edge, *New York Times*, April 19, 2007. Copyright 2007 the *New York Times*. All rights reserved. Used by permission and protected by the copyright laws of the United States. The printing, copying, redistribution, or retransmission of the material without express written permission is prohibited.

23. Neal Gabler, *Walt Disney: The Triumph of the American Imagination* (New York: Knopf, 2006).

24. The Walt Disney Co., annual and quarterly reports, 2006 and 2007.

25. The Walt Disney Co., PowerPoint presentation, "Disney in China," September 22, 2005.

26. Iger presentation, September 10, 2007.

27. Ibid.; "Disney in China"; Merissa Marr, "Disney Rewrites Script to Win Fans in India," *Wall Street Journal*, June 11, 2007; according to the *Census of India 2001*, 363.6 million individuals (35.3 percent of the population) were fourteen or younger, http://www.censusindia.gov.in/Census_And_You/age_structure_and_marital_status.aspx.

28. Iger presentation, September 10, 2007; author's interview with Michael Cieply, November 9, 2007.

29. Author's interview with Trish Lindsay, October 2006; and Star Farm Productions, online at http://www.starfarmproductions.com.

30. Author's interviews with Philip Anschutz and Tim Leiwecke, May 2005; James Flanigan, "Industrialist Who Bid on SFSP: Savvy, Reclusive," *Los Angeles Times*, December 29, 1987, and "Anschutz's Ambitions Are Theatrical," *Los Angeles Times*, February 4, 2001. Copyright 1987 and 2001 *Los Angeles Times*. Reprinted with permission.

Chapter 8

1. Fernand Braudel, *The Perspective of the World* (New York: Harper & Row, 1984); *Forbes*, "As I See It," interview with Fernand Braudel, July 1981.

2. Los Angeles County Economic Development Corp., "Mid-Year Update, 2007–2008, Economic Forecast and Industry Outlook," July 2007.

3. Braudel, *Perspective of the World*, p. 30.

4. California Department of finance, Demographic Reports, Projections, online at http://www.dof.ca.gov.

5. Author's interview with Kevin Starr, 2004.

6. For more information about Murphy, see Margaret Leslie Davis, *The Culture Broker: Franklin D. Murphy and the Transformation of Los Angeles* (Berkeley: University of California Press, 2007).

7. Riordan quoted in Peter H. King and Mark Arax, "As Dynasty Evolved, So Did Power in L.A.," *Los Angeles Times*, March 26, 2006. Copyright 2006 *Los Angeles Times*. Reprinted with permission.

8. Christopher Goffard, "Isolated in Our Cars but Suffering Together," *Los Angeles Times*, June 8, 2008. Copyright 2008 *Los Angeles Times*. Reprinted with permission.

9. Los Angeles County Economic Development Corp., "Economic Forecast, 2008–2009: Mid-Year Update for California and Southern California including the National and International Setting," July 2008, pp. 27–32 (Outlook for Los Angeles County), pp. 32–35 (Outlook for Orange County), pp. 44–47 (Outlook for San Diego County), online at http://www.laedc.org/reports/Forecast-2008-07.pdf.

10. See San Pedro Bay Ports Clean Air Action Plan, online at http://www.clean airactionplan.org.

11. John Husing, presentation to the California Trucking Industry, "Economics of Southern California's Logistics Industry," June 1, 2007.

12. Author's interview with Gray Davis, April 28, 2008, at Milken Institute Global Conference.

13. David Fleming, "Building Successful and Sustainable Public-Private Partnerships for the Future of Los Angeles," panel discussion at Milken Institute Global Conference, April 28, 2008.

14. Husing presentation; author's interview with William F. Lyte, December 2007; "Building a Maritime Technology Cluster at the San Pedro Bay Ports," Kennedy/Jenks Consultants, December 2007, pp. 1–15.

15. For more information on the region's airports, see Los Angeles World Airports, LAX Regional Plan, online at http://www.lawa.org; David Kelly, "San Bernardino Airport May See flights Next Year," *Los Angeles Times*, September 24, 2007; James Flanigan, "Regional Airports Likely Destination for LAX Overflow," *Los Angeles Times*, July 26, 2001, and "Outcome Foggy," *Los Angeles Times*, December 7, 2000. Copyright 2001 and 2000 *Los Angeles Times*. Reprinted with permission.

16. California Department of finance, Demographic Reports, Projections.

17. Author's interview with Eli Broad, 2003; for more information, see The Broad Foundations, online at http://www.broadfoundation.org.

18. California Department of Education, DataQuest, county-level "graduates" data for Los Angeles County, available at http://dq.cde.ca.gov/Dataquest.

19. California Department of Education, DataQuest, county-level "dropouts by grade, ethnicity" data for Orange and San Diego counties, available at http://dq.cde.ca.gov/Dataquest.

20. Author's interviews with Liam Joyce and Judy Ivie Burton, December 2005 and January 2006; James Flanigan, "Venture Capitalists Are Investing in Educational Reform," Entrepreneurial Edge, *New York Times*, February 16, 2006. Copyright 2006 the *New York Times*. All rights reserved. Used by permission and protected by the copyright laws of the United States. The printing, copying, redistribution, or retransmission of the material without express written permission is prohibited.

21. Author's interviews with John Doerr, Theodore Mitchell, Michael Piscal, and Brian Taylor, January 2006; Flanigan, "Venture Capitalists."

22. Mount St. Mary's College Website at http://www.msmc.la.edu; author's interview with Monica Arellano, March 2007.

23. Department of finance, Demographic Reports, Projections.

24. Population Dynamics Research Group, "California Demographic Futures," February 2005, School of Policy, Planning, and Development, University of Southern California, online at http://www.usc.edu.

25. James Flanigan, "Small Businesses Offer Alternatives to Gang Life," Entrepreneurial Edge, *New York Times*, March 20, 2008. Copyright 2008 the *New York Times*. All rights reserved. Used by permission and protected by the copyright laws of the United States. The printing, copying, redistribution, or retransmission of the material without express written permission is prohibited.

26. Polling Report, on immigration, USA Today/Gallup Polls, April 13–15, 2007, LA Times/Bloomberg Poll, April 5–9, 2007, online at http://www.pollingreport.com.

27. See Scott Ratzan, J. Gregory Payne, and Jim Connor, *Tom Bradley: The Impossible Dream* (Santa Monica: Roundtable, 1986).

28. Kevin Starr, *Coast of Dreams: California on the Edge, 1990–2003* (New York: Knopf, 2004), pp. 230, 631.

Index

Italic page numbers indicate illustrations.